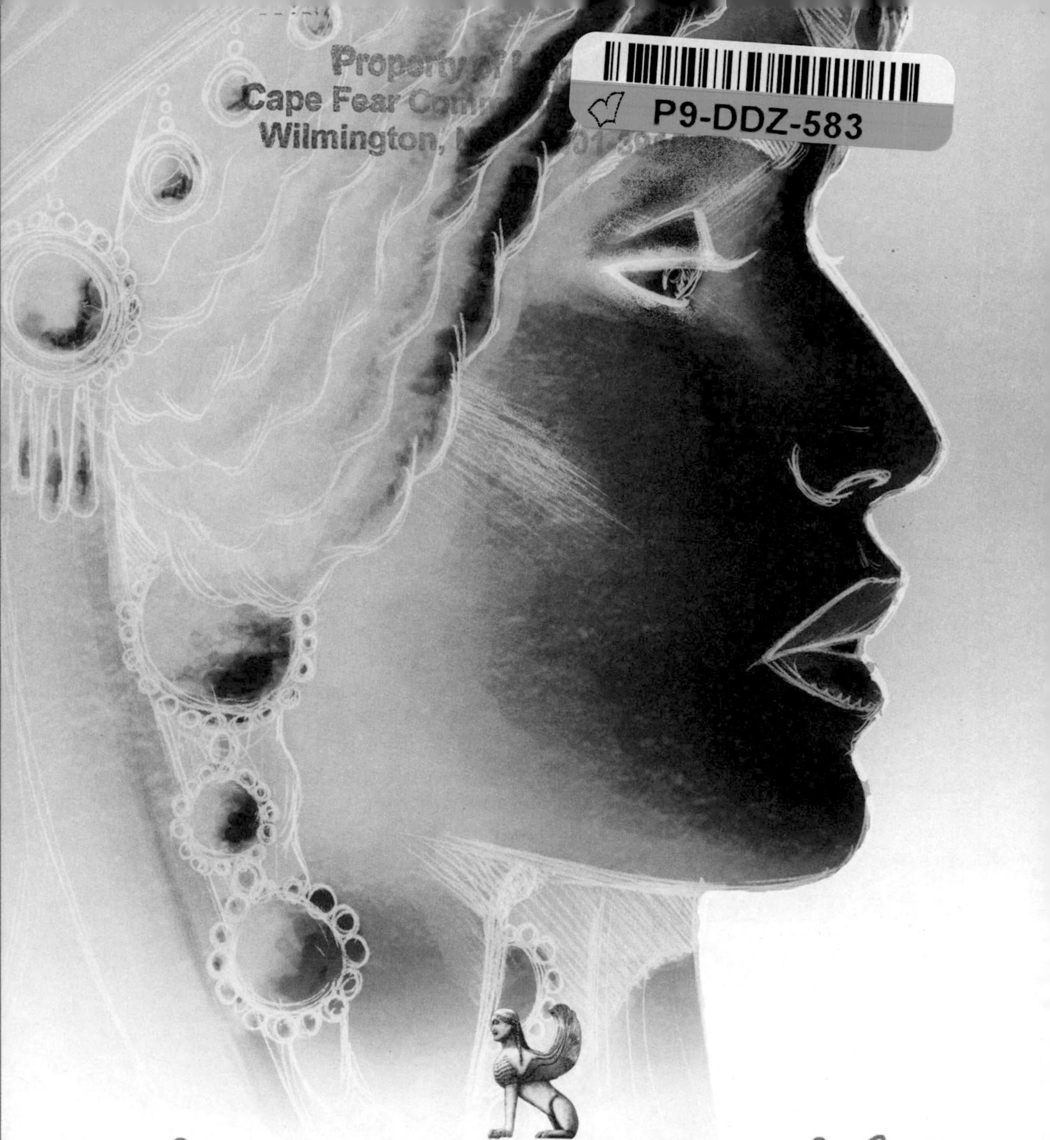

PANDORA'S BOX

VOLUME 3
GLUTTONY

Drawing
STEVEN DUPRÉ

Script
ALCANTE

Colour work
USAGI

9th CINEBOOK
The 9th Art Publisher

Theseus and the Minotaur

The Minotaur was a half-man, half-bull monster, born of the wife of Minos (king of Crete) and a white bull. Minos locked him up inside a labyrinth, where he fed on human flesh. For, each year, the king of Athens, Aegeus, was forced to send seven young men and seven young women to Crete, to be devoured by the Minotaur. Hiding among them, Theseus, son of Aegeus, succeeded in killing the minotaur, then exited the labyrinth by following a string given by Ariadne, daughter of Minos.

Pandora's Box

Of Pride, like Narcissus, you will pay the heavy price.
Of Sloth, like Paris, you will succumb to the slow venom.
Of Gluttony, like Theseus, you will know the foul torment.
Of Lust, like Orpheus, you will bite the bitter fruit.
Of Greed, like Midas, you will learn the hard law.
Of Envy, like Prometheus, you will suffer the eternal punishment.
Of Wrath, like Pandora, you will be the fatal instrument.

Finally, at the very end,
Your soul seven times destroyed,
Only hope will remain,
To live and rise again.

Thus spoke the Oracle
When the box was opened
And its savage spice
Into the world had spread.

Original title: Pandora Box 3 – La Gourmandise
Original edition: © Dupuis, 2005 by Dupré & Alcante
www.dupuis.com
All rights reserved
English translation: © 2009 Cinebook Ltd
Translator: Jerome Saincantin
Lettering and text layout: Imadjinn
Printed in Spain by Just Colour Graphic
This edition first published in Great Britain in 2010 by
Cinebook Ltd
56 Beech Avenue
Canterbury, Kent
CT4 7TA
www.cinebook.com
A CIP catalogue record for this book
is available from the British Library
ISBN 978-1-84918-019-1

9th CINEBOOK
The 9th Art Publisher

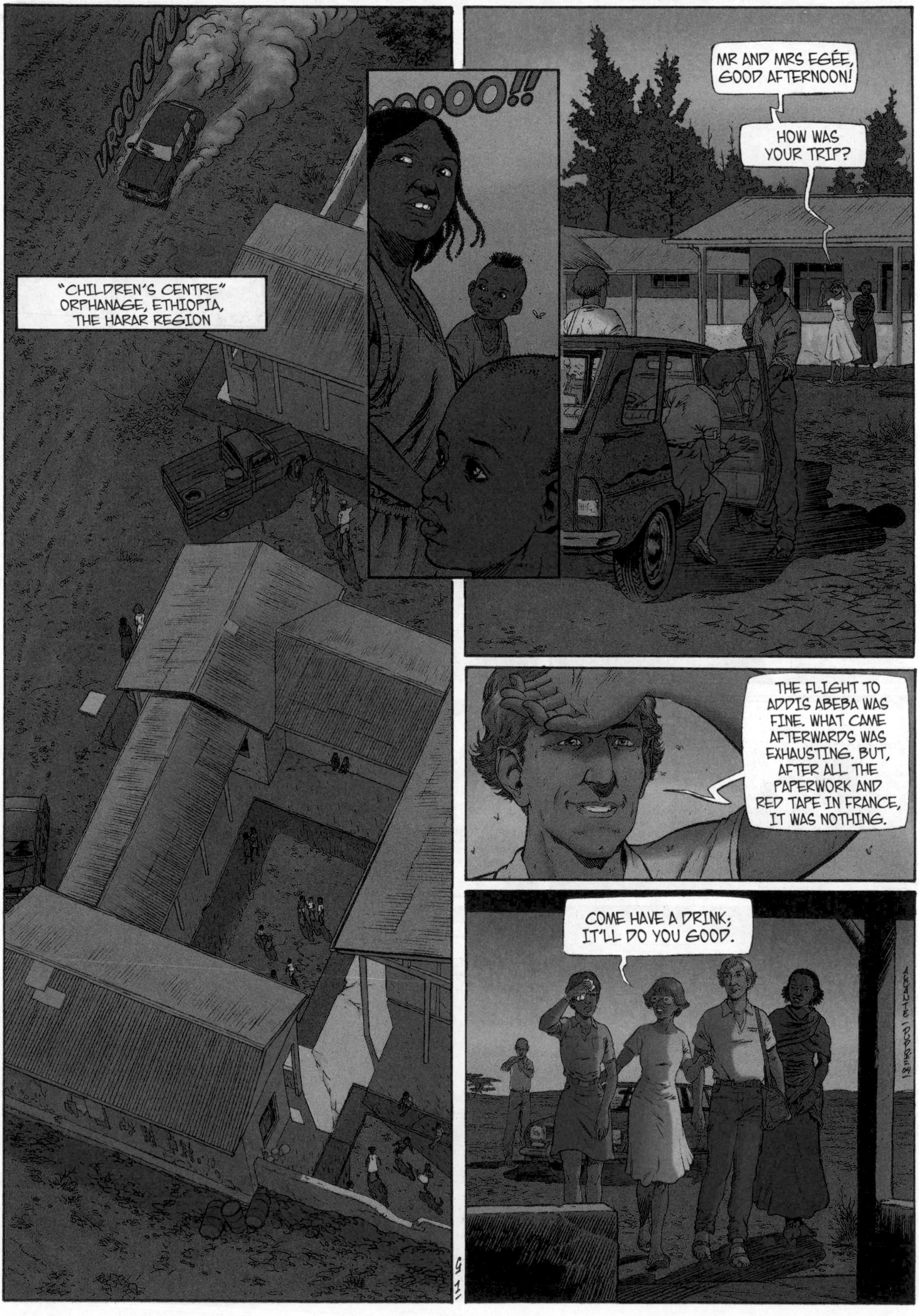
"CHILDREN'S CENTRE" ORPHANAGE, ETHIOPIA, THE HARAR REGION
OOOOO!!
MR AND MRS EGÉE, GOOD AFTERNOON!
HOW WAS YOUR TRIP?
THE FLIGHT TO ADDIS ABEBA WAS FINE. WHAT CAME AFTERWARDS WAS EXHAUSTING. BUT, AFTER ALL THE PAPERWORK AND RED TAPE IN FRANCE, IT WAS NOTHING.
COME HAVE A DRINK; IT'LL DO YOU GOOD.

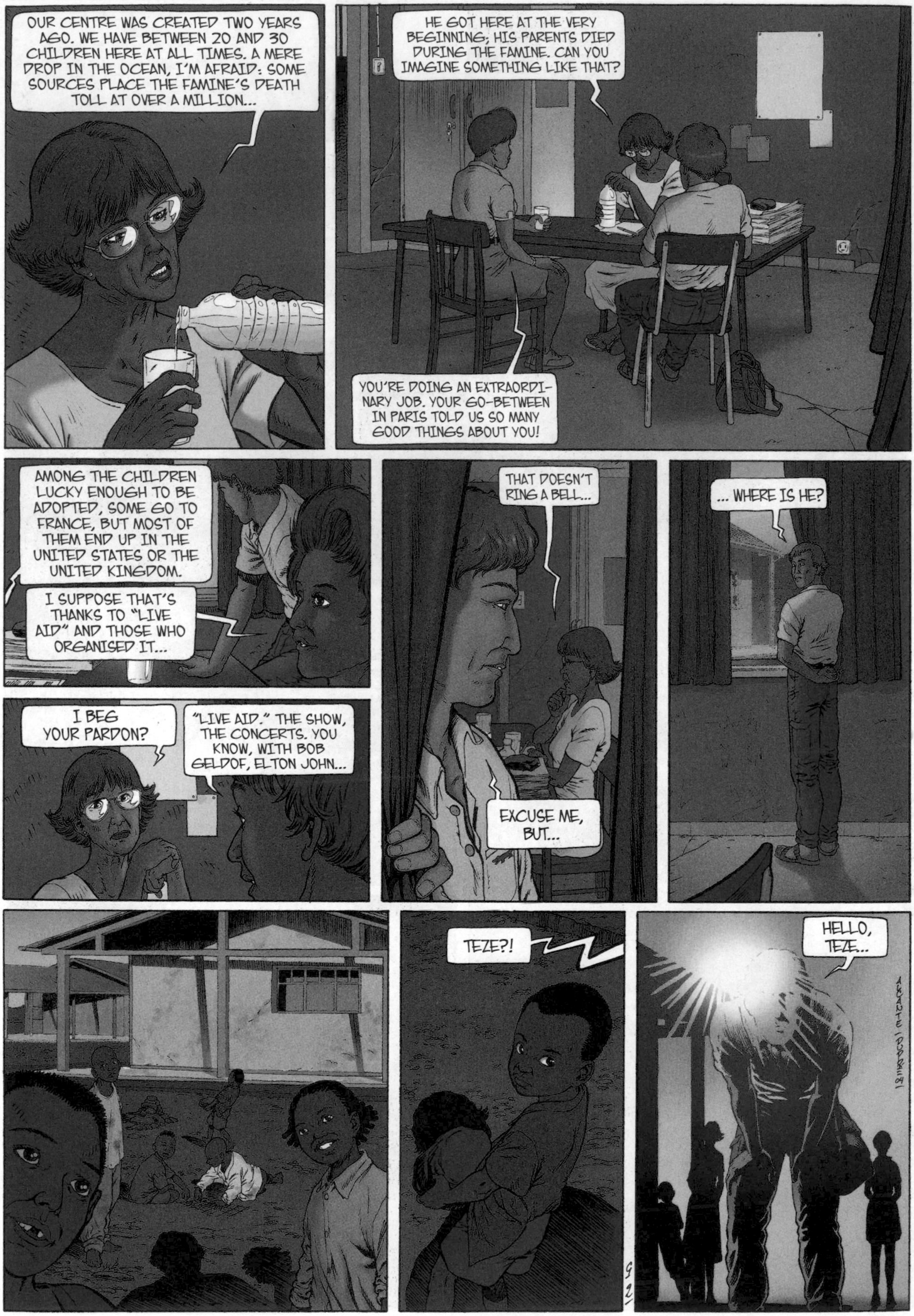
OUR CENTRE WAS CREATED TWO YEARS AGO. WE HAVE BETWEEN 20 AND 30 CHILDREN HERE AT ALL TIMES. A MERE DROP IN THE OCEAN, I'M AFRAID: SOME SOURCES PLACE THE FAMINE'S DEATH TOLL AT OVER A MILLION...
HE GOT HERE AT THE VERY BEGINNING; HIS PARENTS DIED DURING THE FAMINE. CAN YOU IMAGINE SOMETHING LIKE THAT?
YOU'RE DOING AN EXTRAORDI-NARY JOB. YOUR GO-BETWEEN IN PARIS TOLD US SO MANY GOOD THINGS ABOUT YOU!
AMONG THE CHILDREN LUCKY ENOUGH TO BE ADOPTED, SOME GO TO FRANCE, BUT MOST OF THEM END UP IN THE UNITED STATES OR THE UNITED KINGDOM.
I SUPPOSE THAT'S THANKS TO "LIVE AID" AND THOSE WHO ORGANISED IT...
I BEG YOUR PARDON?
"LIVE AID." THE SHOW, THE CONCERTS. YOU KNOW, WITH BOB GELDOF, ELTON JOHN...
THAT DOESN'T RING A BELL...
EXCUSE ME, BUT...
... WHERE IS HE?
TEZE?!
HELLO, TEZE...

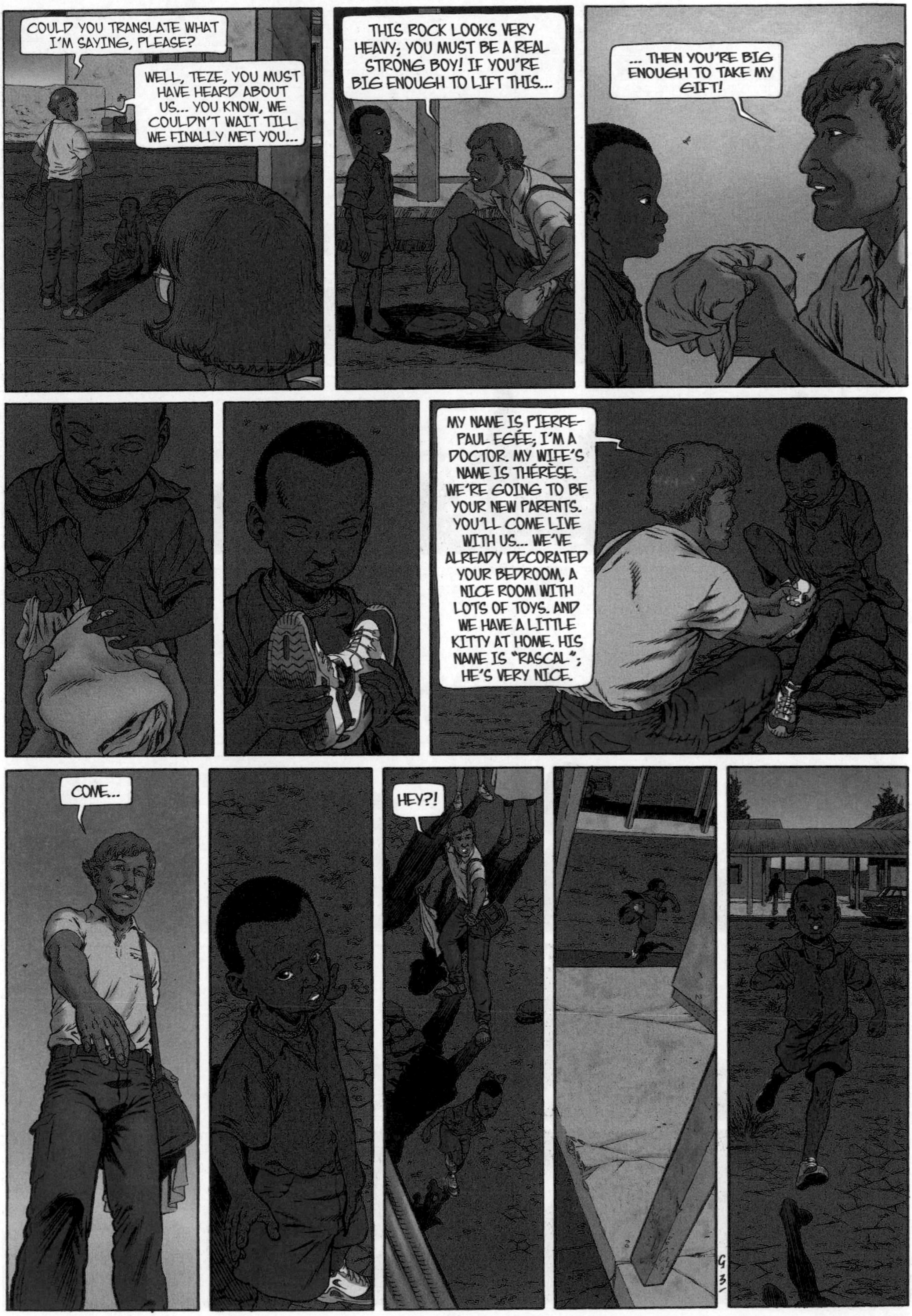
COULD YOU TRANSLATE WHAT I'M SAYING, PLEASE?
WELL, TEZE, YOU MUST HAVE HEARD ABOUT US... YOU KNOW, WE COULDN'T WAIT TILL WE FINALLY MET YOU...
THIS ROCK LOOKS VERY HEAVY; YOU MUST BE A REAL STRONG BOY! IF YOU'RE BIG ENOUGH TO LIFT THIS...
... THEN YOU'RE BIG ENOUGH TO TAKE MY GIFT!
MY NAME IS PIERRE-PAUL EGÉE; I'M A DOCTOR. MY WIFE'S NAME IS THÉRÈSE. WE'RE GOING TO BE YOUR NEW PARENTS. YOU'LL COME LIVE WITH US... WE'VE ALREADY DECORATED YOUR BEDROOM, A NICE ROOM WITH LOTS OF TOYS. AND WE HAVE A LITTLE KITTY AT HOME. HIS NAME IS "RASCAL"; HE'S VERY NICE.
COME...
HEY?!

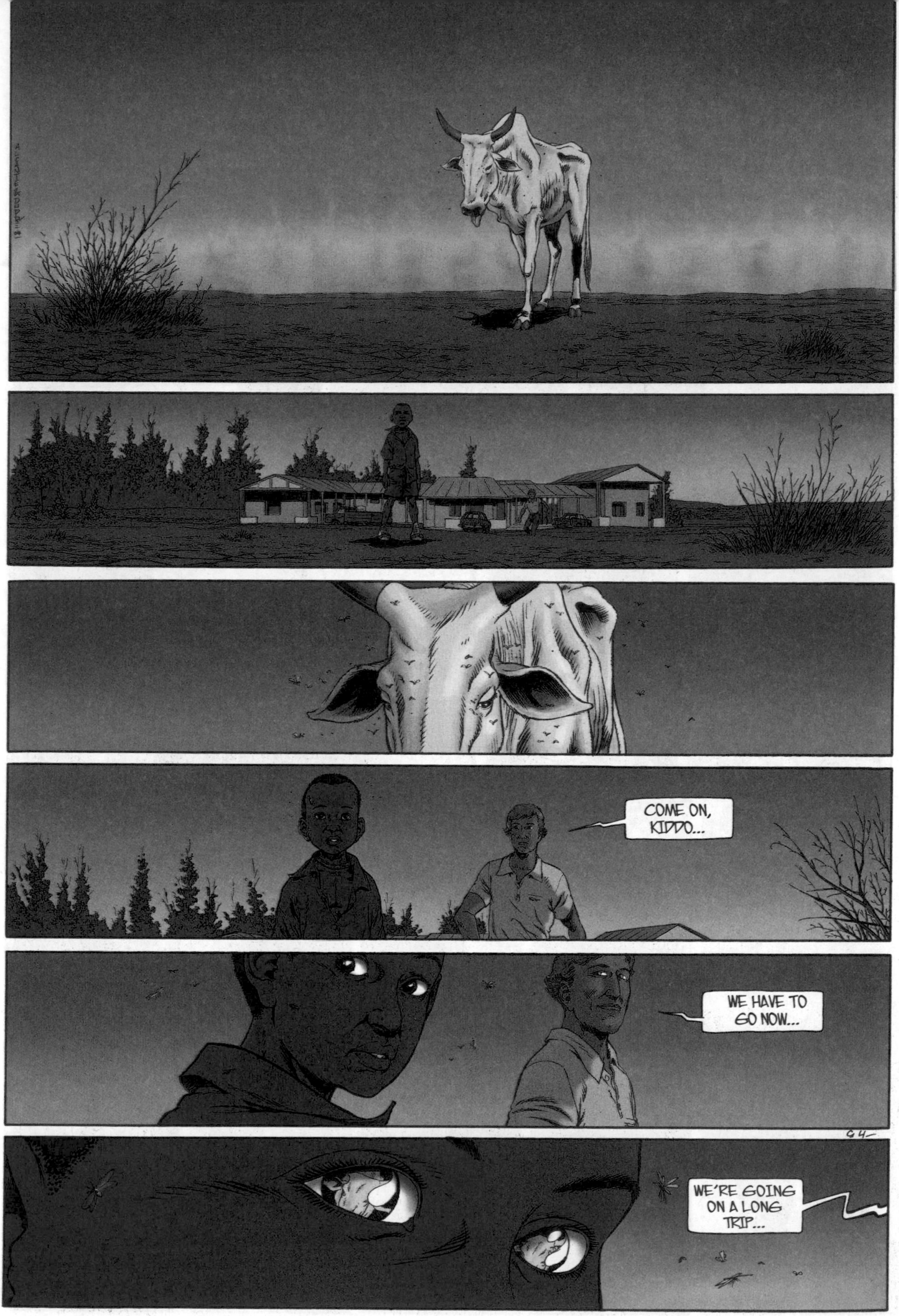
COME ON, KIDDO...
WE HAVE TO GO NOW...
WE'RE GOING ON A LONG TRIP...

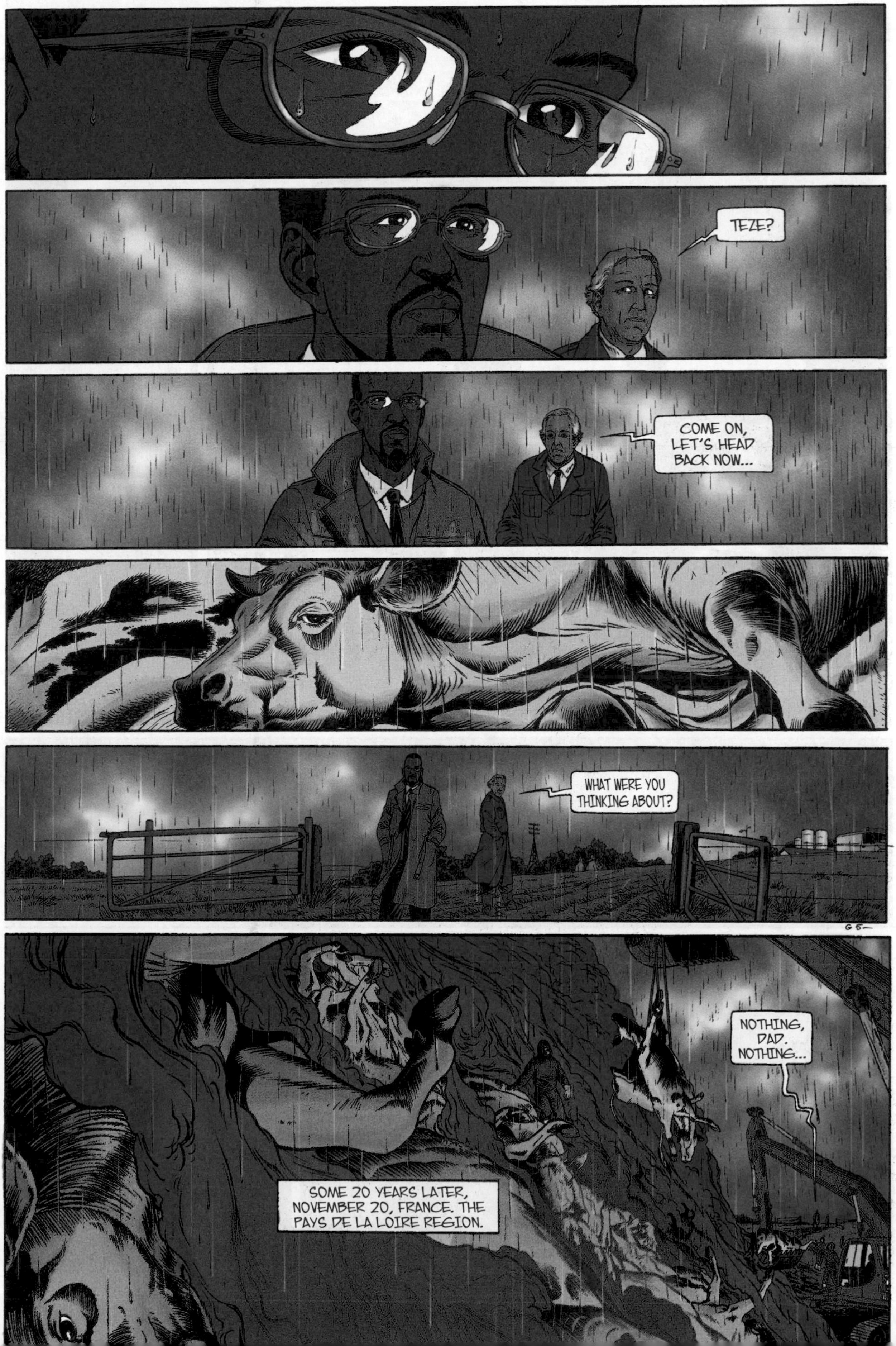
TEZE?
COME ON, LET'S HEAD BACK NOW...
WHAT WERE YOU THINKING ABOUT?
SOME 20 YEARS LATER, NOVEMBER 20, FRANCE. THE PAYS DE LA LOIRE REGION.
NOTHING, DAD. NOTHING...

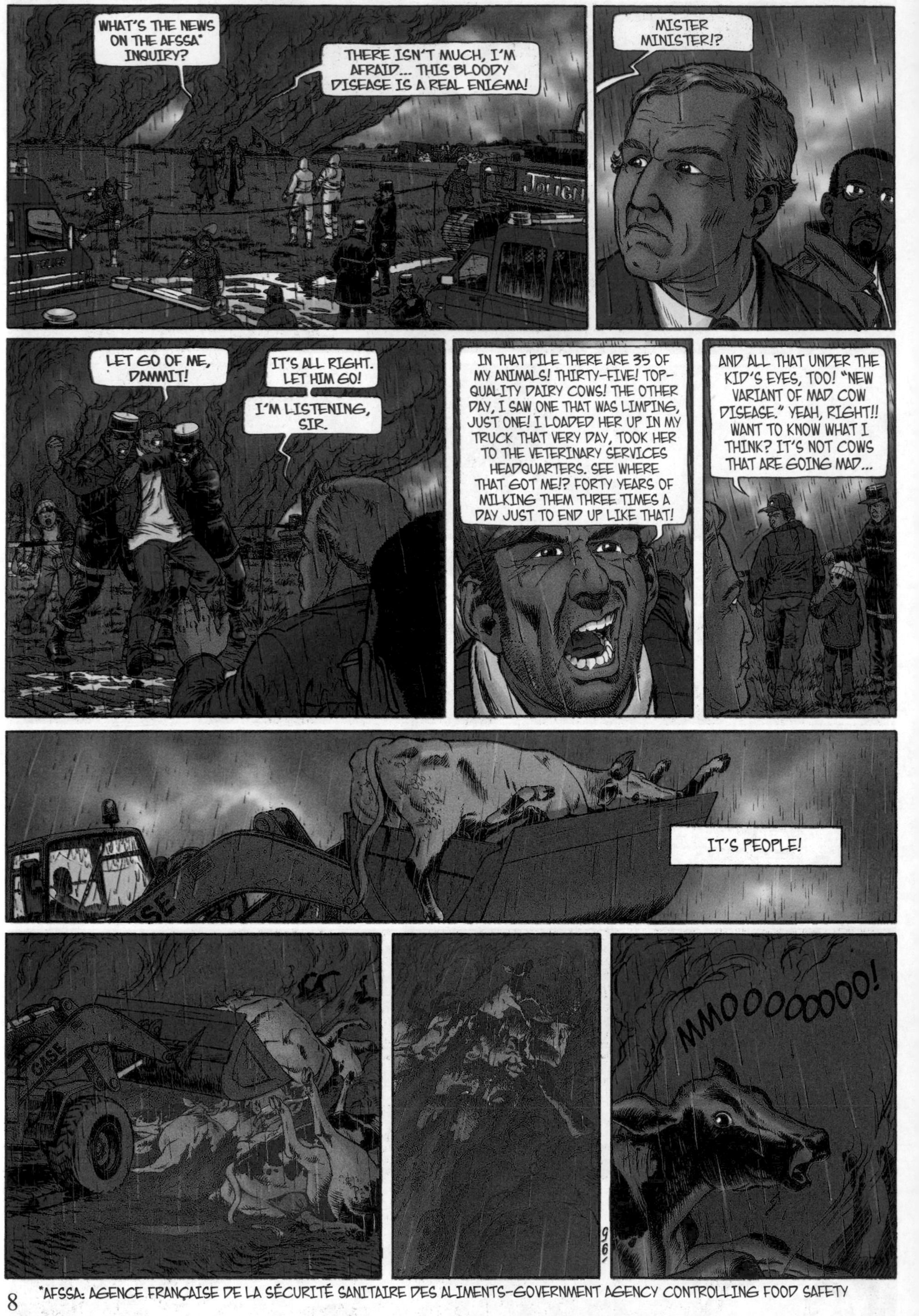
WHAT'S THE NEWS ON THE AFSSA* INQUIRY?
THERE ISN'T MUCH, I'M AFRAID... THIS BLOODY DISEASE IS A REAL ENIGMA!
MISTER MINISTER!?
LET GO OF ME, DAMMIT!
IT'S ALL RIGHT. LET HIM GO!
I'M LISTENING, SIR.
IN THAT PILE THERE ARE 35 OF MY ANIMALS! THIRTY-FIVE! TOP-QUALITY DAIRY COWS! THE OTHER DAY, I SAW ONE THAT WAS LIMPING, JUST ONE! I LOADED HER UP IN MY TRUCK THAT VERY DAY, TOOK HER TO THE VETERINARY SERVICES HEADQUARTERS. SEE WHERE THAT GOT ME!? FORTY YEARS OF MILKING THEM THREE TIMES A DAY JUST TO END UP LIKE THAT!
AND ALL THAT UNDER THE KID'S EYES, TOO! "NEW VARIANT OF MAD COW DISEASE." YEAH, RIGHT!! WANT TO KNOW WHAT I THINK? IT'S NOT COWS THAT ARE GOING MAD...
IT'S PEOPLE!
MMOOOOOOOO!

*AFSSA: AGENCE FRANÇAISE DE LA SÉCURITÉ SANITAIRE DES ALIMENTS–GOVERNMENT AGENCY CONTROLLING FOOD SAFETY

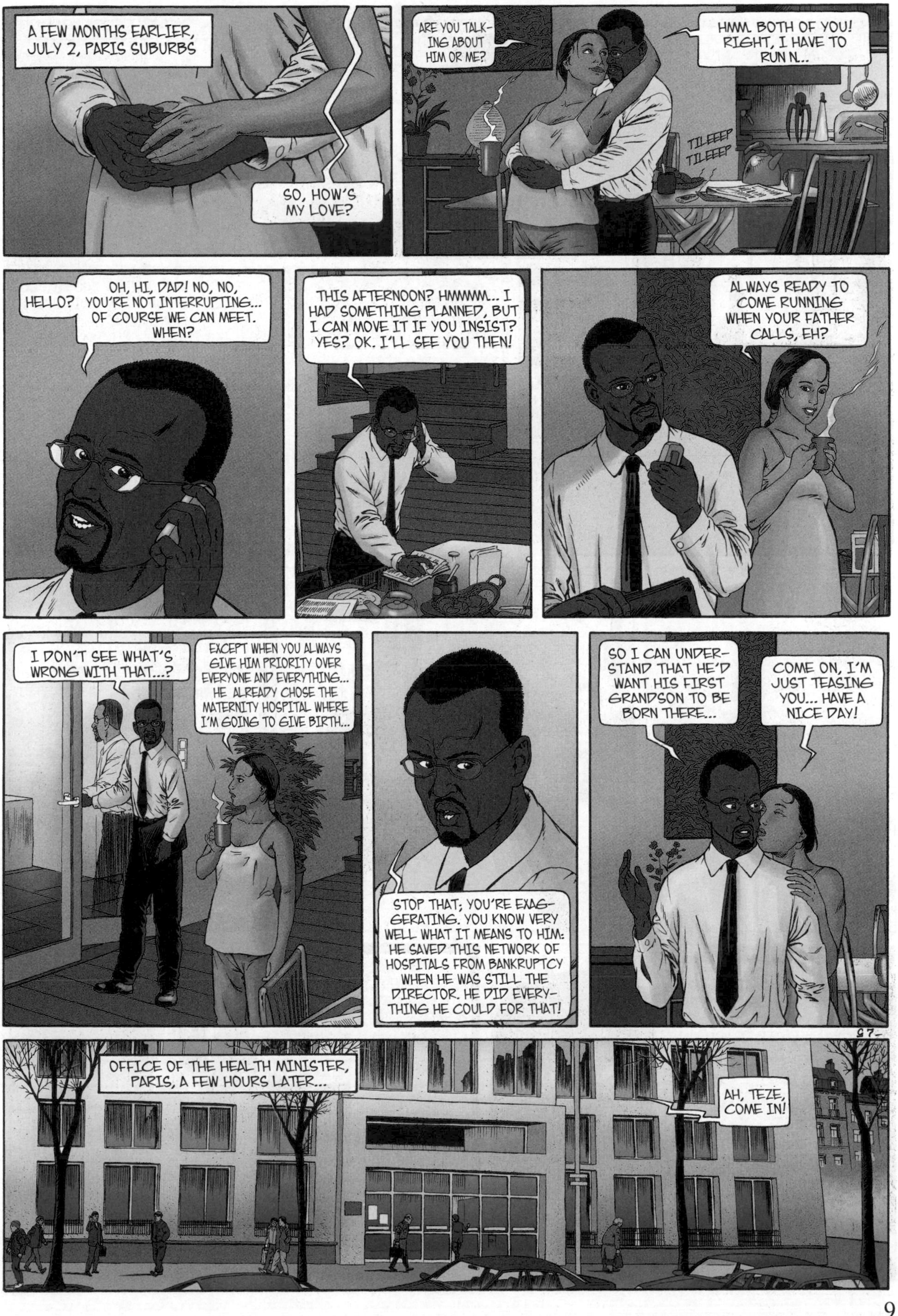

A FEW MONTHS EARLIER, JULY 2, PARIS SUBURBS
SO, HOW'S MY LOVE?
ARE YOU TALKING ABOUT HIM OR ME?
HMM. BOTH OF YOU! RIGHT, I HAVE TO RUN N...
TILEEEP TILEEEP
HELLO?
OH, HI, DAD! NO, NO, YOU'RE NOT INTERRUPTING... OF COURSE WE CAN MEET. WHEN?
THIS AFTERNOON? HMMMM... I HAD SOMETHING PLANNED, BUT I CAN MOVE IT IF YOU INSIST? YES? OK. I'LL SEE YOU THEN!
ALWAYS READY TO COME RUNNING WHEN YOUR FATHER CALLS, EH?
I DON'T SEE WHAT'S WRONG WITH THAT...?
EXCEPT WHEN YOU ALWAYS GIVE HIM PRIORITY OVER EVERYONE AND EVERYTHING... HE ALREADY CHOSE THE MATERNITY HOSPITAL WHERE I'M GOING TO GIVE BIRTH...
STOP THAT; YOU'RE EXAGGERATING. YOU KNOW VERY WELL WHAT IT MEANS TO HIM: HE SAVED THIS NETWORK OF HOSPITALS FROM BANKRUPTCY WHEN HE WAS STILL THE DIRECTOR. HE DID EVERYTHING HE COULD FOR THAT!
SO I CAN UNDERSTAND THAT HE'D WANT HIS FIRST GRANDSON TO BE BORN THERE...
COME ON, I'M JUST TEASING YOU... HAVE A NICE DAY!
OFFICE OF THE HEALTH MINISTER, PARIS, A FEW HOURS LATER...
AH, TEZE, COME IN!

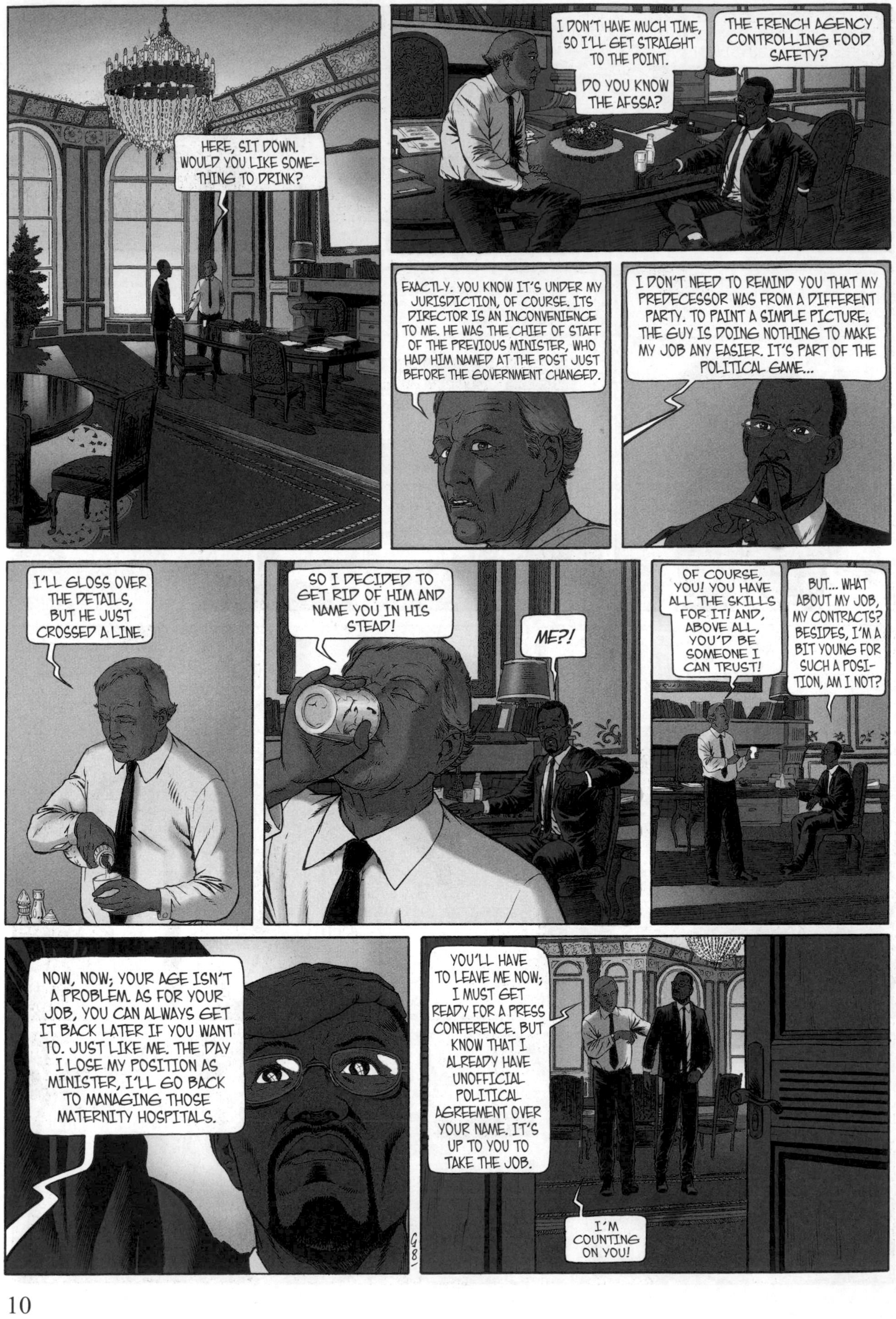
HERE, SIT DOWN. WOULD YOU LIKE SOMETHING TO DRINK?
I DON'T HAVE MUCH TIME, SO I'LL GET STRAIGHT TO THE POINT.
DO YOU KNOW THE AFSSA?
THE FRENCH AGENCY CONTROLLING FOOD SAFETY?
EXACTLY. YOU KNOW IT'S UNDER MY JURISDICTION, OF COURSE. ITS DIRECTOR IS AN INCONVENIENCE TO ME. HE WAS THE CHIEF OF STAFF OF THE PREVIOUS MINISTER, WHO HAD HIM NAMED AT THE POST JUST BEFORE THE GOVERNMENT CHANGED.
I DON'T NEED TO REMIND YOU THAT MY PREDECESSOR WAS FROM A DIFFERENT PARTY. TO PAINT A SIMPLE PICTURE: THE GUY IS DOING NOTHING TO MAKE MY JOB ANY EASIER. IT'S PART OF THE POLITICAL GAME...
I'LL GLOSS OVER THE DETAILS, BUT HE JUST CROSSED A LINE.
SO I DECIDED TO GET RID OF HIM AND NAME YOU IN HIS STEAD!
ME?!
OF COURSE, YOU! YOU HAVE ALL THE SKILLS FOR IT! AND, ABOVE ALL, YOU'D BE SOMEONE I CAN TRUST!
BUT... WHAT ABOUT MY JOB, MY CONTRACTS? BESIDES, I'M A BIT YOUNG FOR SUCH A POSITION, AM I NOT?
NOW, NOW; YOUR AGE ISN'T A PROBLEM. AS FOR YOUR JOB, YOU CAN ALWAYS GET IT BACK LATER IF YOU WANT TO. JUST LIKE ME. THE DAY I LOSE MY POSITION AS MINISTER, I'LL GO BACK TO MANAGING THOSE MATERNITY HOSPITALS.
YOU'LL HAVE TO LEAVE ME NOW; I MUST GET READY FOR A PRESS CONFERENCE. BUT KNOW THAT I ALREADY HAVE UNOFFICIAL POLITICAL AGREEMENT OVER YOUR NAME. IT'S UP TO YOU TO TAKE THE JOB.
I'M COUNTING ON YOU!

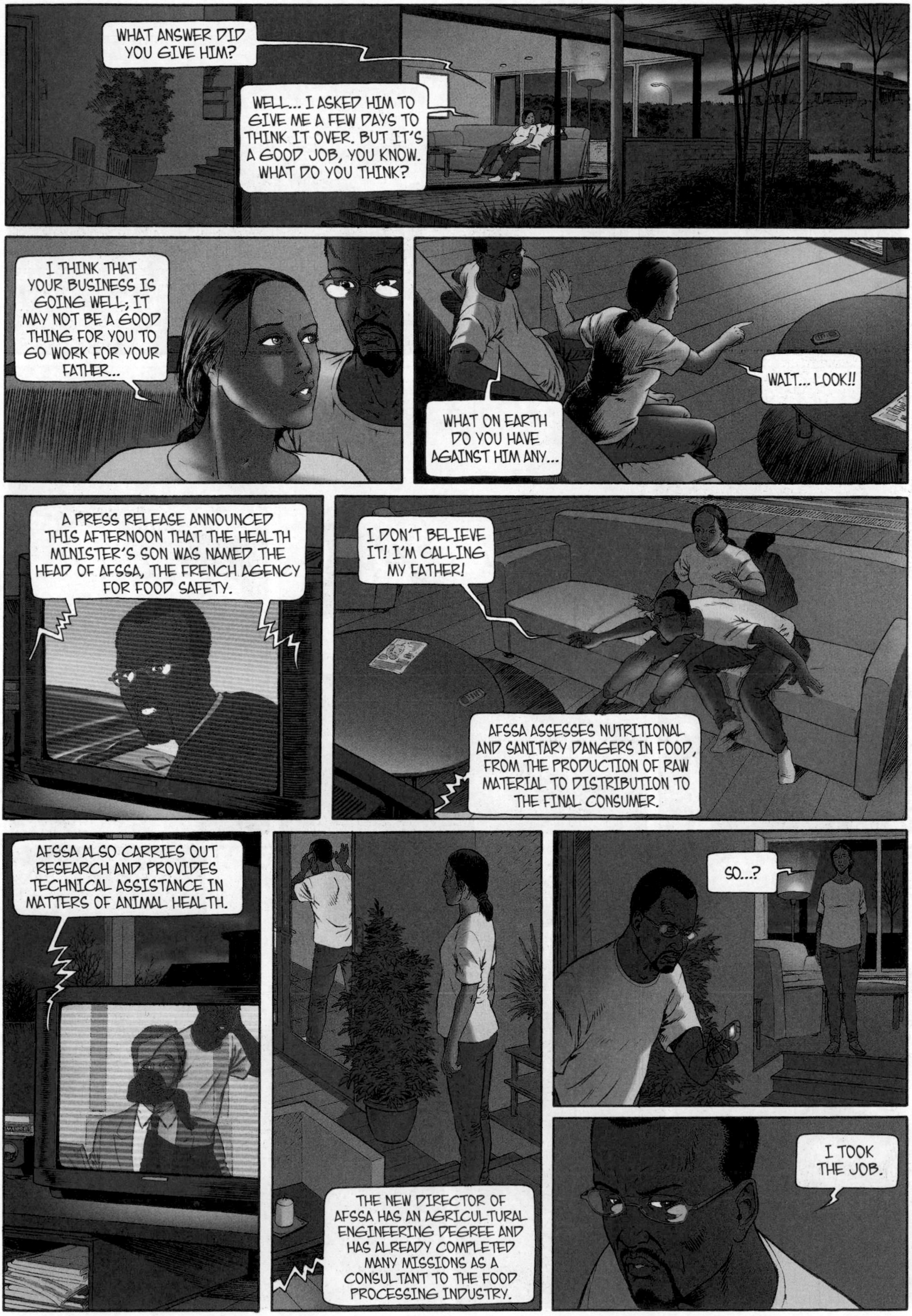

WHAT ANSWER DID YOU GIVE HIM?
WELL... I ASKED HIM TO GIVE ME A FEW DAYS TO THINK IT OVER. BUT IT'S A GOOD JOB, YOU KNOW. WHAT DO YOU THINK?
I THINK THAT YOUR BUSINESS IS GOING WELL; IT MAY NOT BE A GOOD THING FOR YOU TO GO WORK FOR YOUR FATHER...
WHAT ON EARTH DO YOU HAVE AGAINST HIM ANY...
WAIT... LOOK!!
A PRESS RELEASE ANNOUNCED THIS AFTERNOON THAT THE HEALTH MINISTER'S SON WAS NAMED THE HEAD OF AFSSA, THE FRENCH AGENCY FOR FOOD SAFETY.
I DON'T BELIEVE IT! I'M CALLING MY FATHER!
AFSSA ASSESSES NUTRITIONAL AND SANITARY DANGERS IN FOOD, FROM THE PRODUCTION OF RAW MATERIAL TO DISTRIBUTION TO THE FINAL CONSUMER.
AFSSA ALSO CARRIES OUT RESEARCH AND PROVIDES TECHNICAL ASSISTANCE IN MATTERS OF ANIMAL HEALTH.
THE NEW DIRECTOR OF AFSSA HAS AN AGRICULTURAL ENGINEERING DEGREE AND HAS ALREADY COMPLETED MANY MISSIONS AS A CONSULTANT TO THE FOOD PROCESSING INDUSTRY.
SO...?
I TOOK THE JOB.

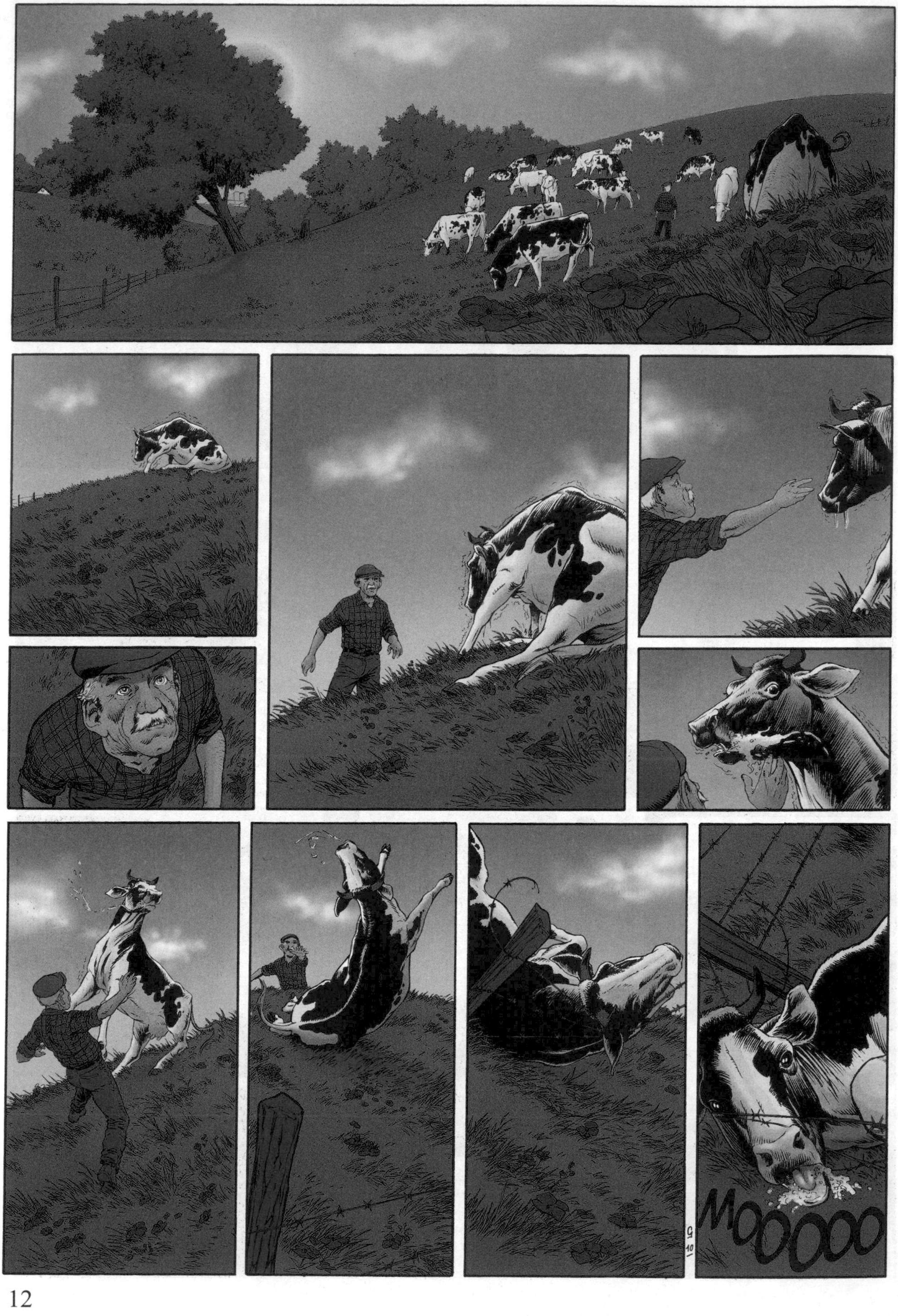
MOOOOO

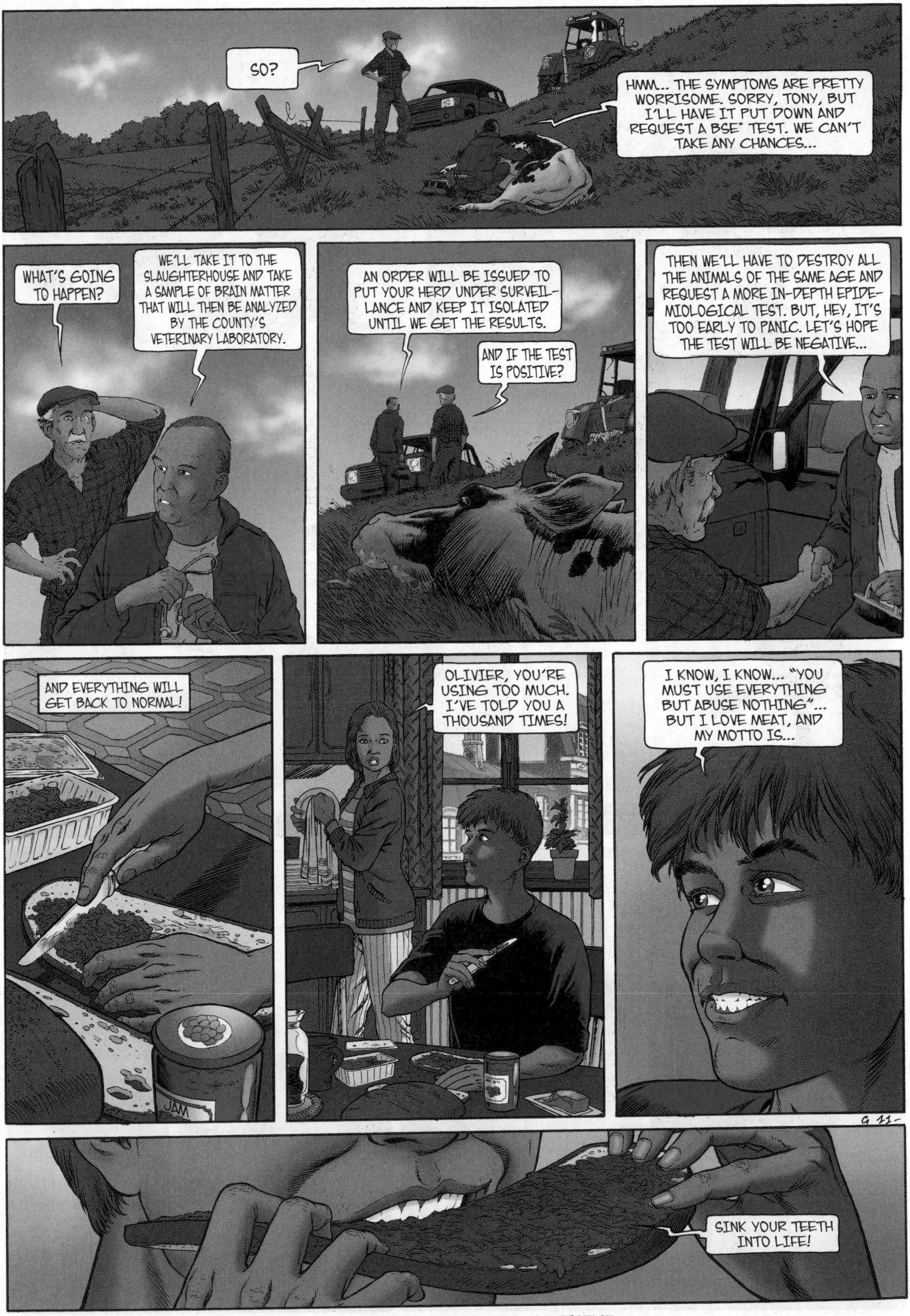
SO?
HMM... THE SYMPTOMS ARE PRETTY WORRISOME. SORRY, TONY, BUT I'LL HAVE IT PUT DOWN AND REQUEST A BSE* TEST. WE CAN'T TAKE ANY CHANCES...
WHAT'S GOING TO HAPPEN?
WE'LL TAKE IT TO THE SLAUGHTERHOUSE AND TAKE A SAMPLE OF BRAIN MATTER THAT WILL THEN BE ANALYZED BY THE COUNTY'S VETERINARY LABORATORY.
AN ORDER WILL BE ISSUED TO PUT YOUR HERD UNDER SURVEIL-LANCE AND KEEP IT ISOLATED UNTIL WE GET THE RESULTS.
AND IF THE TEST IS POSITIVE?
THEN WE'LL HAVE TO DESTROY ALL THE ANIMALS OF THE SAME AGE AND REQUEST A MORE IN-DEPTH EPIDE-MIOLOGICAL TEST. BUT, HEY, IT'S TOO EARLY TO PANIC. LET'S HOPE THE TEST WILL BE NEGATIVE...
AND EVERYTHING WILL GET BACK TO NORMAL!
JAM
OLIVIER, YOU'RE USING TOO MUCH. I'VE TOLD YOU A THOUSAND TIMES!
I KNOW, I KNOW... "YOU MUST USE EVERYTHING BUT ABUSE NOTHING"... BUT I LOVE MEAT, AND MY MOTTO IS...
SINK YOUR TEETH INTO LIFE!

*BOVINE SPONGIFORM ENCEPHALOPATHY, THE SCIENTIFIC NAME OF MAD COW DISEASE

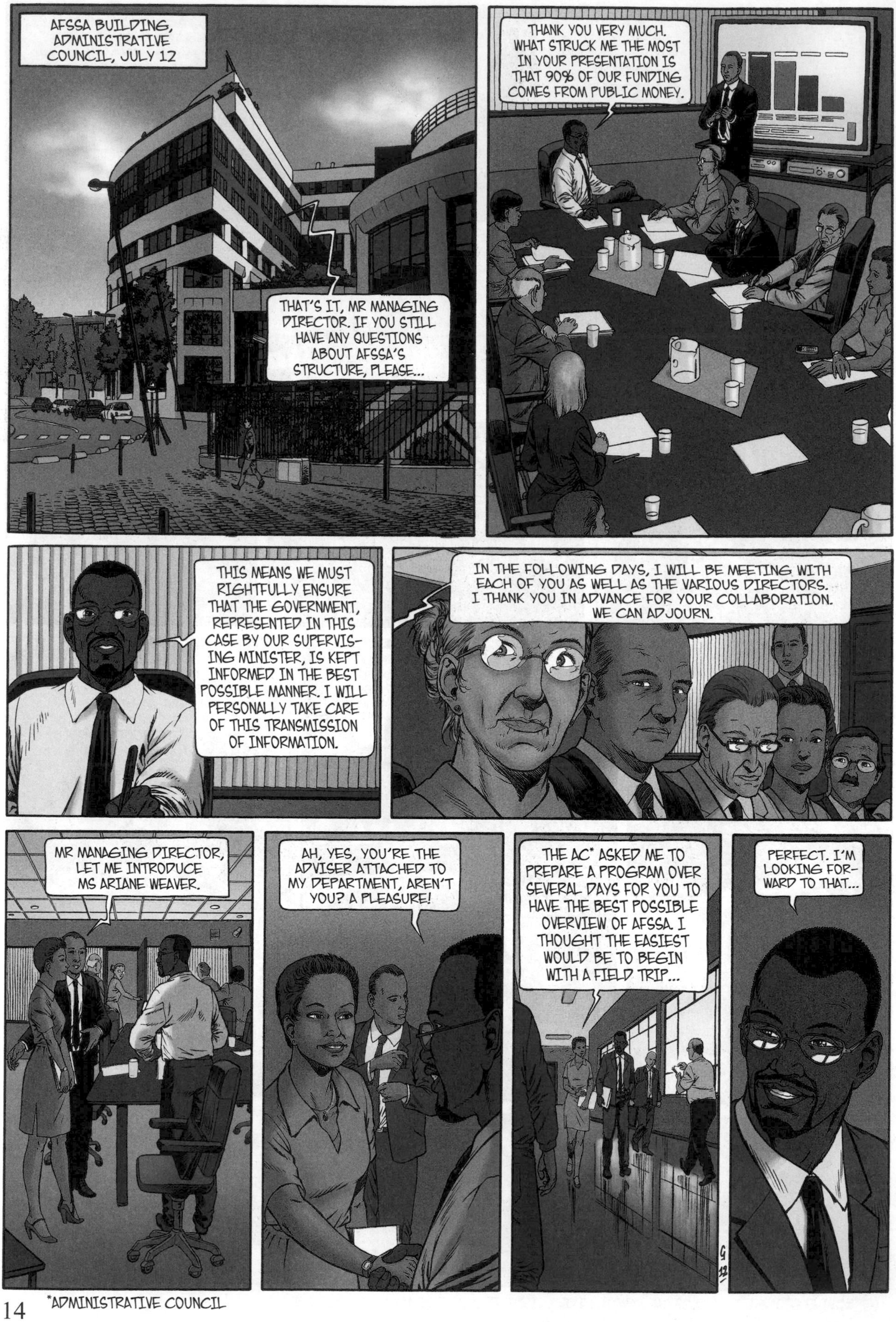
AFSSA BUILDING, ADMINISTRATIVE COUNCIL, JULY 12
THAT'S IT, MR MANAGING DIRECTOR. IF YOU STILL HAVE ANY QUESTIONS ABOUT AFSSA'S STRUCTURE, PLEASE...
THANK YOU VERY MUCH. WHAT STRUCK ME THE MOST IN YOUR PRESENTATION IS THAT 90% OF OUR FUNDING COMES FROM PUBLIC MONEY.
THIS MEANS WE MUST RIGHTFULLY ENSURE THAT THE GOVERNMENT, REPRESENTED IN THIS CASE BY OUR SUPERVISING MINISTER, IS KEPT INFORMED IN THE BEST POSSIBLE MANNER. I WILL PERSONALLY TAKE CARE OF THIS TRANSMISSION OF INFORMATION.
IN THE FOLLOWING DAYS, I WILL BE MEETING WITH EACH OF YOU AS WELL AS THE VARIOUS DIRECTORS. I THANK YOU IN ADVANCE FOR YOUR COLLABORATION. WE CAN ADJOURN.
MR MANAGING DIRECTOR, LET ME INTRODUCE MS ARIANE WEAVER.
AH, YES, YOU'RE THE ADVISER ATTACHED TO MY DEPARTMENT, AREN'T YOU? A PLEASURE!
THE AC* ASKED ME TO PREPARE A PROGRAM OVER SEVERAL DAYS FOR YOU TO HAVE THE BEST POSSIBLE OVERVIEW OF AFSSA. I THOUGHT THE EASIEST WOULD BE TO BEGIN WITH A FIELD TRIP...
PERFECT. I'M LOOKING FORWARD TO THAT...

*ADMINISTRATIVE COUNCIL

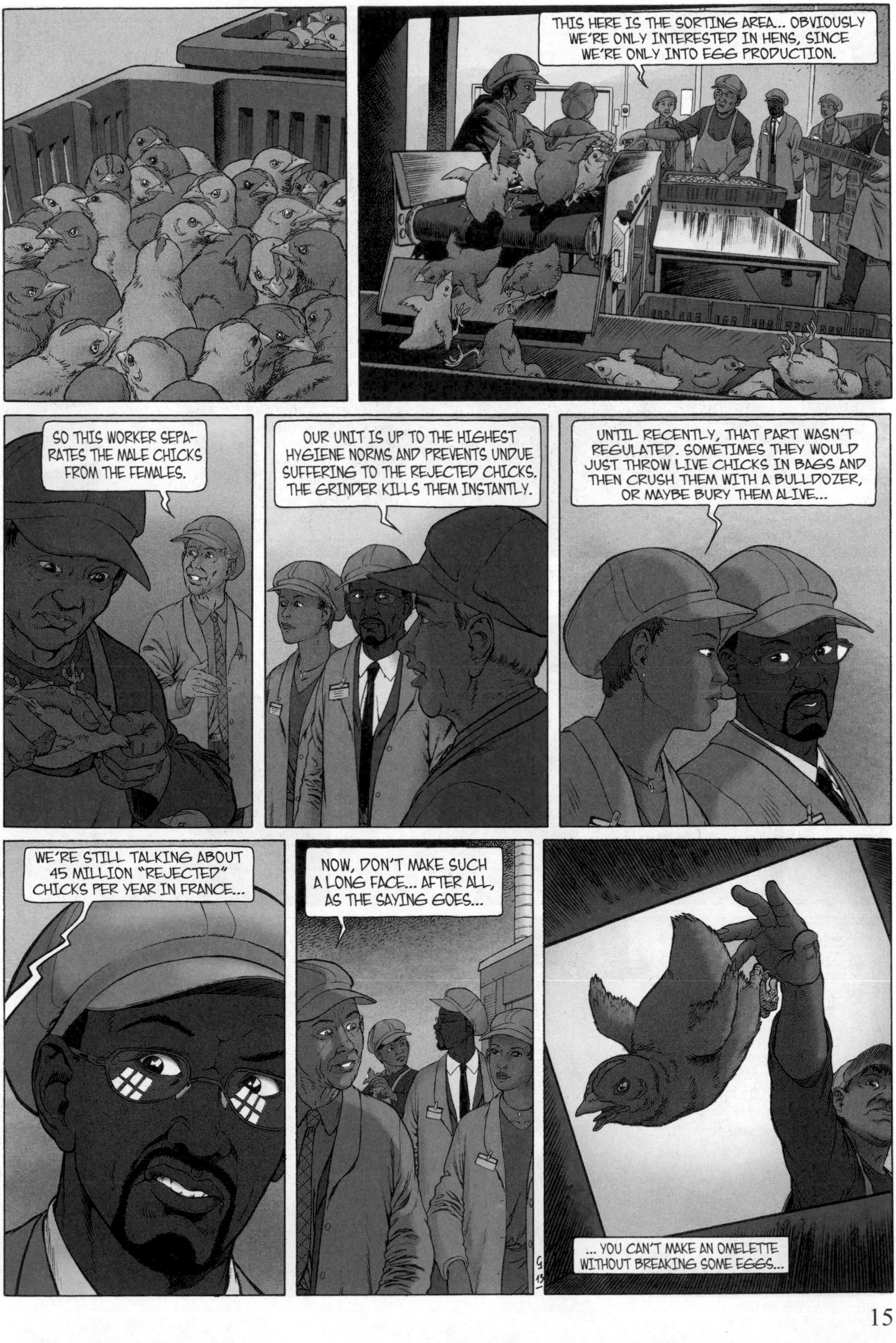
THIS HERE IS THE SORTING AREA... OBVIOUSLY WE'RE ONLY INTERESTED IN HENS, SINCE WE'RE ONLY INTO EGG PRODUCTION.
SO THIS WORKER SEPARATES THE MALE CHICKS FROM THE FEMALES.
OUR UNIT IS UP TO THE HIGHEST HYGIENE NORMS AND PREVENTS UNDUE SUFFERING TO THE REJECTED CHICKS. THE GRINDER KILLS THEM INSTANTLY.
UNTIL RECENTLY, THAT PART WASN'T REGULATED. SOMETIMES THEY WOULD JUST THROW LIVE CHICKS IN BAGS AND THEN CRUSH THEM WITH A BULLDOZER, OR MAYBE BURY THEM ALIVE...
WE'RE STILL TALKING ABOUT 45 MILLION "REJECTED" CHICKS PER YEAR IN FRANCE...
NOW, DON'T MAKE SUCH A LONG FACE... AFTER ALL, AS THE SAYING GOES...
... YOU CAN'T MAKE AN OMELETTE WITHOUT BREAKING SOME EGGS...

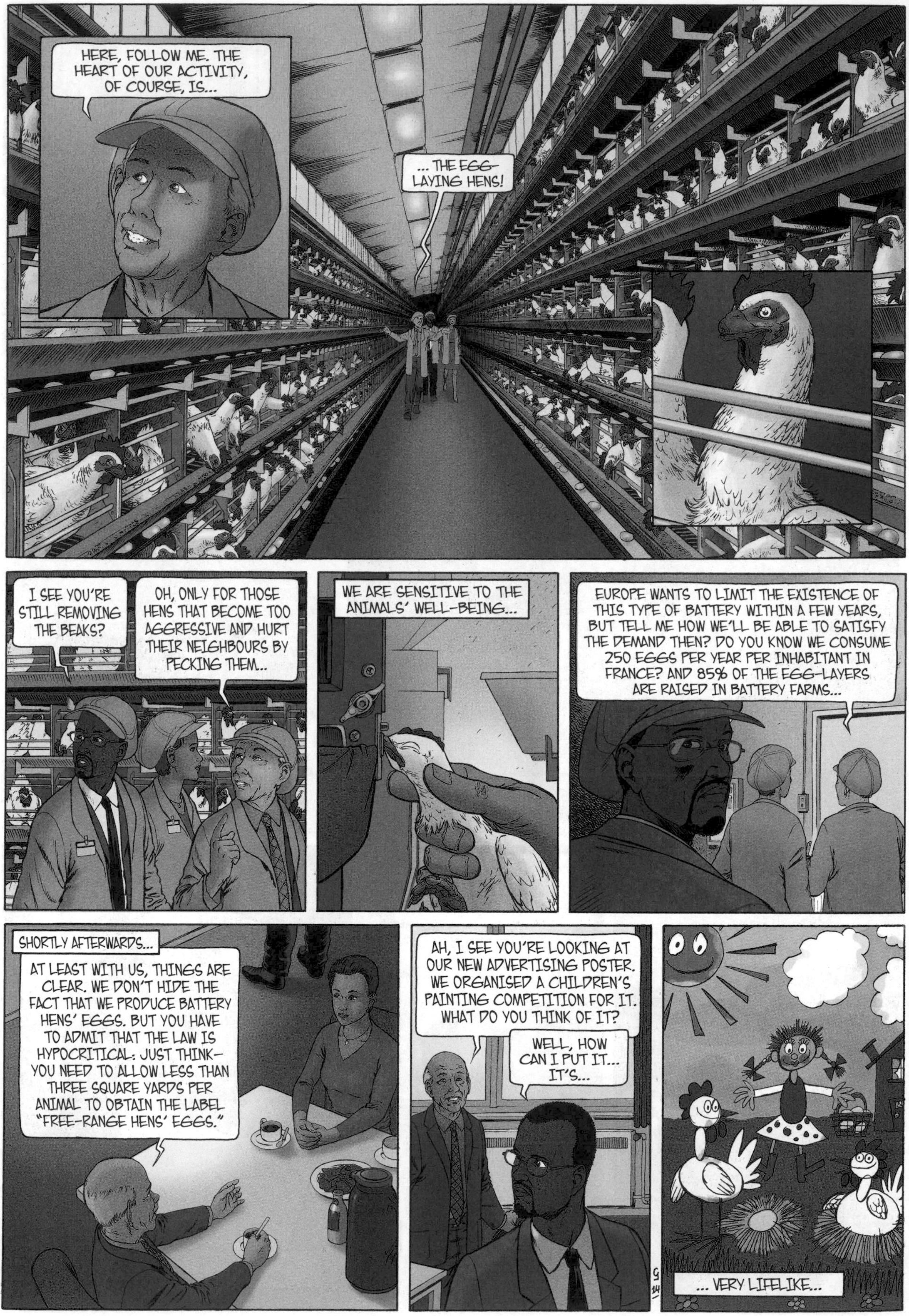

HERE, FOLLOW ME. THE HEART OF OUR ACTIVITY, OF COURSE, IS...
... THE EGG-LAYING HENS!
I SEE YOU'RE STILL REMOVING THE BEAKS?
OH, ONLY FOR THOSE HENS THAT BECOME TOO AGGRESSIVE AND HURT THEIR NEIGHBOURS BY PECKING THEM...
WE ARE SENSITIVE TO THE ANIMALS' WELL-BEING...
EUROPE WANTS TO LIMIT THE EXISTENCE OF THIS TYPE OF BATTERY WITHIN A FEW YEARS, BUT TELL ME HOW WE'LL BE ABLE TO SATISFY THE DEMAND THEN? DO YOU KNOW WE CONSUME 250 EGGS PER YEAR PER INHABITANT IN FRANCE? AND 85% OF THE EGG-LAYERS ARE RAISED IN BATTERY FARMS...
SHORTLY AFTERWARDS...
AT LEAST WITH US, THINGS ARE CLEAR. WE DON'T HIDE THE FACT THAT WE PRODUCE BATTERY HENS' EGGS. BUT YOU HAVE TO ADMIT THAT THE LAW IS HYPOCRITICAL: JUST THINK-YOU NEED TO ALLOW LESS THAN THREE SQUARE YARDS PER ANIMAL TO OBTAIN THE LABEL "FREE-RANGE HENS' EGGS."
AH, I SEE YOU'RE LOOKING AT OUR NEW ADVERTISING POSTER. WE ORGANISED A CHILDREN'S PAINTING COMPETITION FOR IT. WHAT DO YOU THINK OF IT?
WELL, HOW CAN I PUT IT... IT'S...
... VERY LIFELIKE...

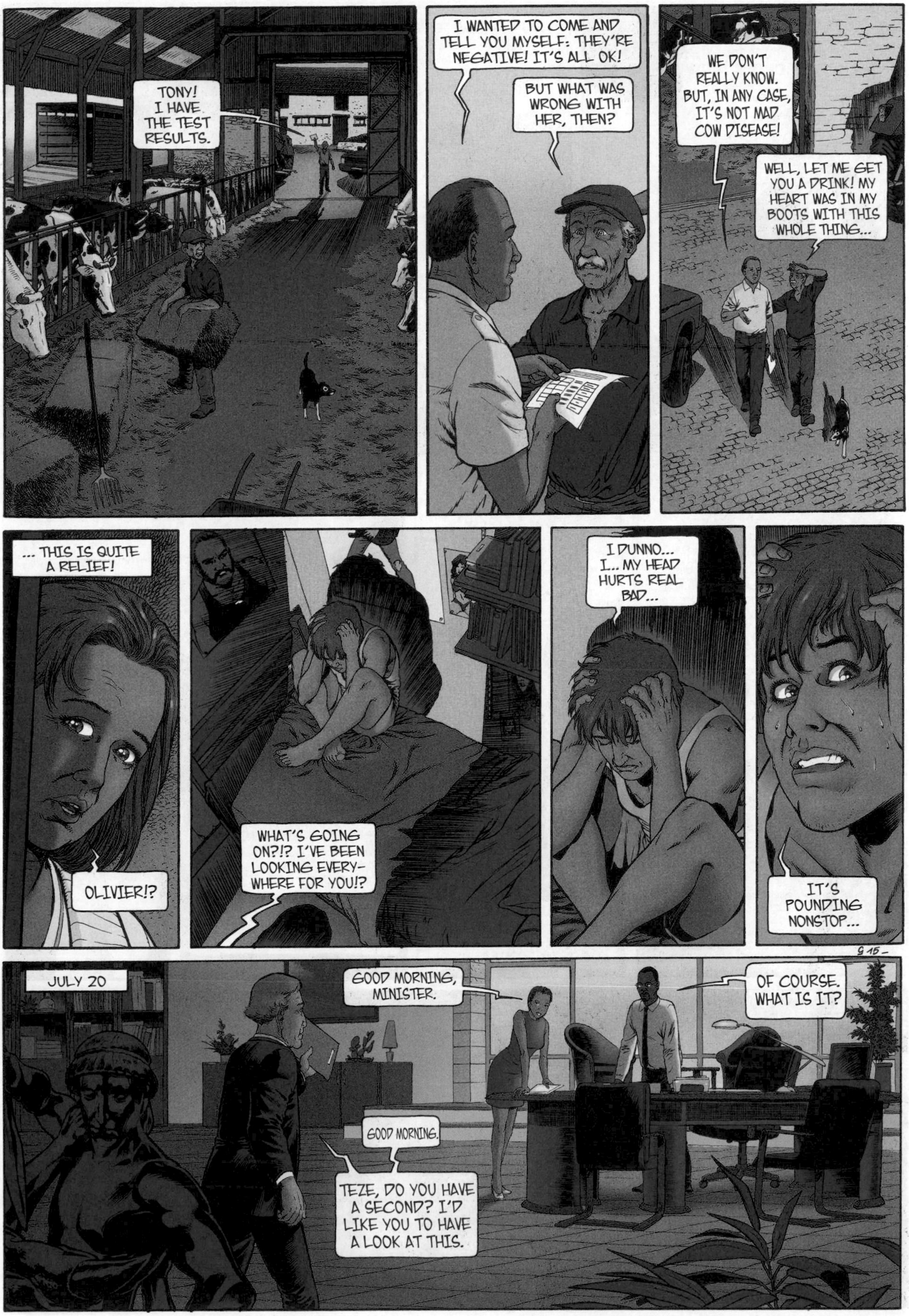
TONY! I HAVE THE TEST RESULTS.
I WANTED TO COME AND TELL YOU MYSELF: THEY'RE NEGATIVE! IT'S ALL OK!
BUT WHAT WAS WRONG WITH HER, THEN?
WE DON'T REALLY KNOW. BUT, IN ANY CASE, IT'S NOT MAD COW DISEASE!
WELL, LET ME GET YOU A DRINK! MY HEART WAS IN MY BOOTS WITH THIS WHOLE THING...
... THIS IS QUITE A RELIEF!
OLIVIER!?
WHAT'S GOING ON?!? I'VE BEEN LOOKING EVERY-WHERE FOR YOU!?
I DUNNO... I... MY HEAD HURTS REAL BAD...
IT'S POUNDING NONSTOP...
JULY 20
GOOD MORNING, MINISTER.
OF COURSE. WHAT IS IT?
GOOD MORNING.
TEZE, DO YOU HAVE A SECOND? I'D LIKE YOU TO HAVE A LOOK AT THIS.

ONE OF THE LAST FILES TRANSMITTED BY YOUR PREDECESSOR. SOMETHING THAT SHOULD BE WATCHED CLOSELY, I THINK.
YOU'VE KNOWN FOR A GOOD WHILE THAT THE NUMBER OF BSE CLINICAL TESTS* HAS STABILISED AT AROUND 10 A MONTH... BUT FOR THE PAST FEW WEEKS NOW, AFSSA HAS NOTICED AN INCREASE IN THIS TYPE OF REQUEST, AND WE HAVE CASES ALL OVER FRANCE.
THAT'S ONE OF THE FILES I HAVE YET TO TALK TO YOU ABOUT.
LOOK. SINCE APRIL, THE NUMBERS HAVE BEEN INCREASING RATHER NOTICEABLY.
TROUBLING?
AT THIS STAGE, NOT YET, FOR THE NUMBER OF POSITIVE TESTS HASN'T INCREASED AT ALL. EVEN IF THEY SHOW SYMPTOMS RESEMBLING THOSE OF MAD COW DISEASE, THESE COWS HAVEN'T CONTRACTED IT.
NONETHELESS, THIS IS STILL DISTURBING! DO NOT TREAT IT LIGHTLY!
OF COURSE NOT! OUR AGENCY IS FOLLOWING THIS FILE VERY CLOSELY, IT GOES WITHOUT SAYING!
BOTTOM LINE, ARIANE?
AS A PRECAUTIONARY MEASURE, WE HAVE REQUESTED MORE ADVANCED TESTS IN CONFIRMATION FOR ALL THE SAMPLES ANALYSED SINCE JANUARY. AND WE'VE SET UP A DATABASE WITH ALL THE EPIDEMIOLOGICAL STATISTICS...
IN ANY CASE, THIS KIND OF NEWS IS NOT TO THE LIKING OF THE AGRICULTURE MINISTER. HE'S DEATHLY AFRAID THAT PEOPLE MIGHT START TALKING ABOUT MAD COW AGAIN... I WOULDN'T BE SURPRISED IF HE CONTACTED YOU TO DISCUSS IT, ACTUALLY!
AH, TEZE, GOOD EVENING!
Le Train Bleu
Restaurant

*CLINICAL TESTS: TESTS APPLIED FOLLOWING A CLINICAL SUSPICION (VET OR FARMER NOTICING SYMPTOMS OF THE DISEASE). THIS NETWORK OF SURVEILLANCE, CALLED "PASSIVE," IS DISTINCT FROM THE "ACTIVE" NETWORK THAT COMPRISES THE SYSTEMATIC TESTING CARRIED OUT IN SLAUGHTERHOUSES.

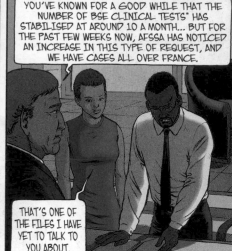

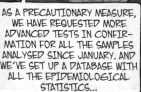

SIT DOWN, PLEASE!

YOU LOOK TIRED, IF YOU DON'T MIND MY SAYING...?

I HAD A BUSY DAY. WE VISITED A BEEF FACTORY FARM... BUT I'M NOT SURE I WANT TO TALK ABOUT IT...

I UNDERSTAND. AS OTTO VON BISMARCK SAID: "LAWS ARE LIKE SAUSAGES. IT IS BEST NOT TO SEE THEM BEING MADE!" TOUGH LUCK FOR ME; AS AGRICULTURE MINISTER, I'M ONE OF THE FEW WHO GETS TO SEE BOTH!

HAVE YOU EVER BEEN HERE BEFORE? I LOVE THIS RESTAURANT. BUT IT'S ALWAYS PACKED; THAT'S THE ONLY DOWNSIDE...

... IT FEELS A BIT CROWDED.

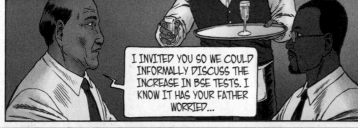

I INVITED YOU SO WE COULD INFORMALLY DISCUSS THE INCREASE IN BSE TESTS. I KNOW IT HAS YOUR FATHER WORRIED...

BUT BEFORE WE BROACH THE SUBJECT, HERE...

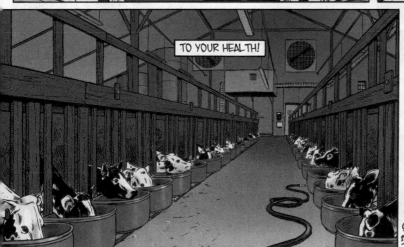

TO YOUR HEALTH!

IT'S CLEAR THAT THE SITUATION HAS TO BE MONITORED CLOSELY, BUT I WOULD ENCOURAGE YOU NOT TO ACT PRECIPITOUSLY, ESPECIALLY IN REGARD TO THE MEDIA, WHO DO NOT ALWAYS PUT THINGS INTO PERSPECTIVE. IT WOULD ONLY TAKE ONE REPORTER CRYING "MAD COW" FOR THE WHOLE INDUSTRY TO GET HIT RIGHT AWAY.

19

WAITER! WAITER!

OH, DEAR, THIS PLACE IS SO BUSY...

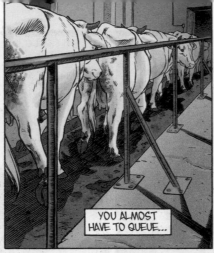

YOU ALMOST HAVE TO QUEUE...

DON'T FORGET THE ECONOMIC IMPORTANCE OF THE BEEF MARKET: WITH 21 MILLION HEAD, FRANCE IS THE MAIN PRODUCER IN EUROPE. IT'S ALSO THE MAIN CONSUMER, WITH 55 POUNDS PER YEAR PER PERSON, EVEN IF THE NUMBER IS CURRENTLY DECREASING...

IT'S STILL 10 TIMES THE TOTAL CONSUMPTION OF MEAT IN INDIA, FOR EXAMPLE...

ER... HAVE YOU CHOSEN? YOU HAVE TO ADMIT THE PRICES ARE...

A BIT OF A SHOCK!

YOU KNOW THERE ARE 278,000 CATTLE FARMS IN FRANCE, AND THE SECTOR'S TURNOVER IS AROUND €60 BILLION. WE MUST AVOID WEAKENING IT NEEDLESSLY WHEN IT'S ALREADY SUFFERED SO MUCH.

YOU'LL SEE; IT'S SO TENDER...

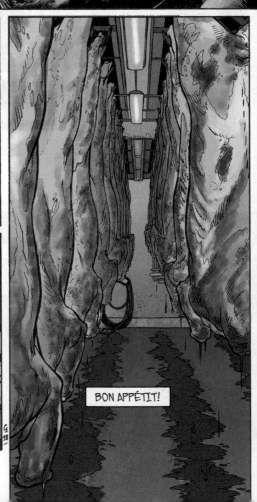

BON APPÉTIT!

20

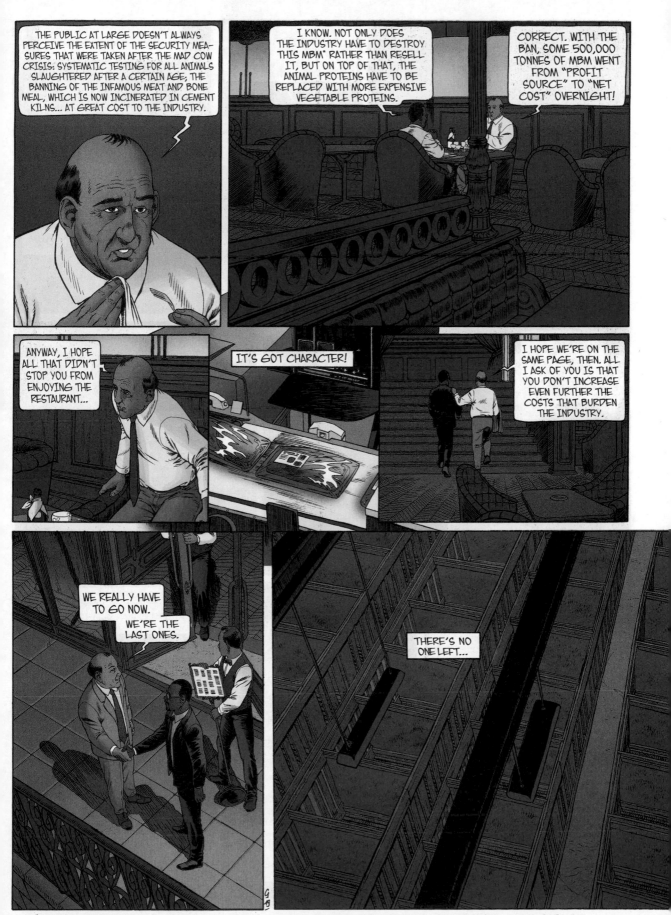

THE PUBLIC AT LARGE DOESN'T ALWAYS PERCEIVE THE EXTENT OF THE SECURITY MEASURES THAT WERE TAKEN AFTER THE MAD COW CRISIS: SYSTEMATIC TESTING FOR ALL ANIMALS SLAUGHTERED AFTER A CERTAIN AGE; THE BANNING OF THE INFAMOUS MEAT AND BONE MEAL, WHICH IS NOW INCINERATED IN CEMENT KILNS... AT GREAT COST TO THE INDUSTRY.

I KNOW. NOT ONLY DOES THE INDUSTRY HAVE TO DESTROY THIS MBM* RATHER THAN RESELL IT, BUT ON TOP OF THAT, THE ANIMAL PROTEINS HAVE TO BE REPLACED WITH MORE EXPENSIVE VEGETABLE PROTEINS.

CORRECT. WITH THE BAN, SOME 500,000 TONNES OF MBM WENT FROM "PROFIT SOURCE" TO "NET COST" OVERNIGHT!

ANYWAY, I HOPE ALL THAT DIDN'T STOP YOU FROM ENJOYING THE RESTAURANT...

IT'S GOT CHARACTER!

I HOPE WE'RE ON THE SAME PAGE, THEN. ALL I ASK OF YOU IS THAT YOU DON'T INCREASE EVEN FURTHER THE COSTS THAT BURDEN THE INDUSTRY.

WE REALLY HAVE TO GO NOW.

WE'RE THE LAST ONES.

THERE'S NO ONE LEFT...

*MEAT AND BONE MEAL IS POWDERED FEED OBTAINED AFTER THE RENDERING OF SLAUGHTERED ANIMAL PARTS. IT IS THE INCORPORATION OF MBM FROM DISEASED ANIMALS INTO CATTLE FEED THAT IS RESPONSIBLE FOR THE SPREAD OF MAD COW DISEASE AND, FROM THERE, OF ITS HUMAN FORM, THE VARIANT CREUTZFELDT–JAKOB DISEASE.

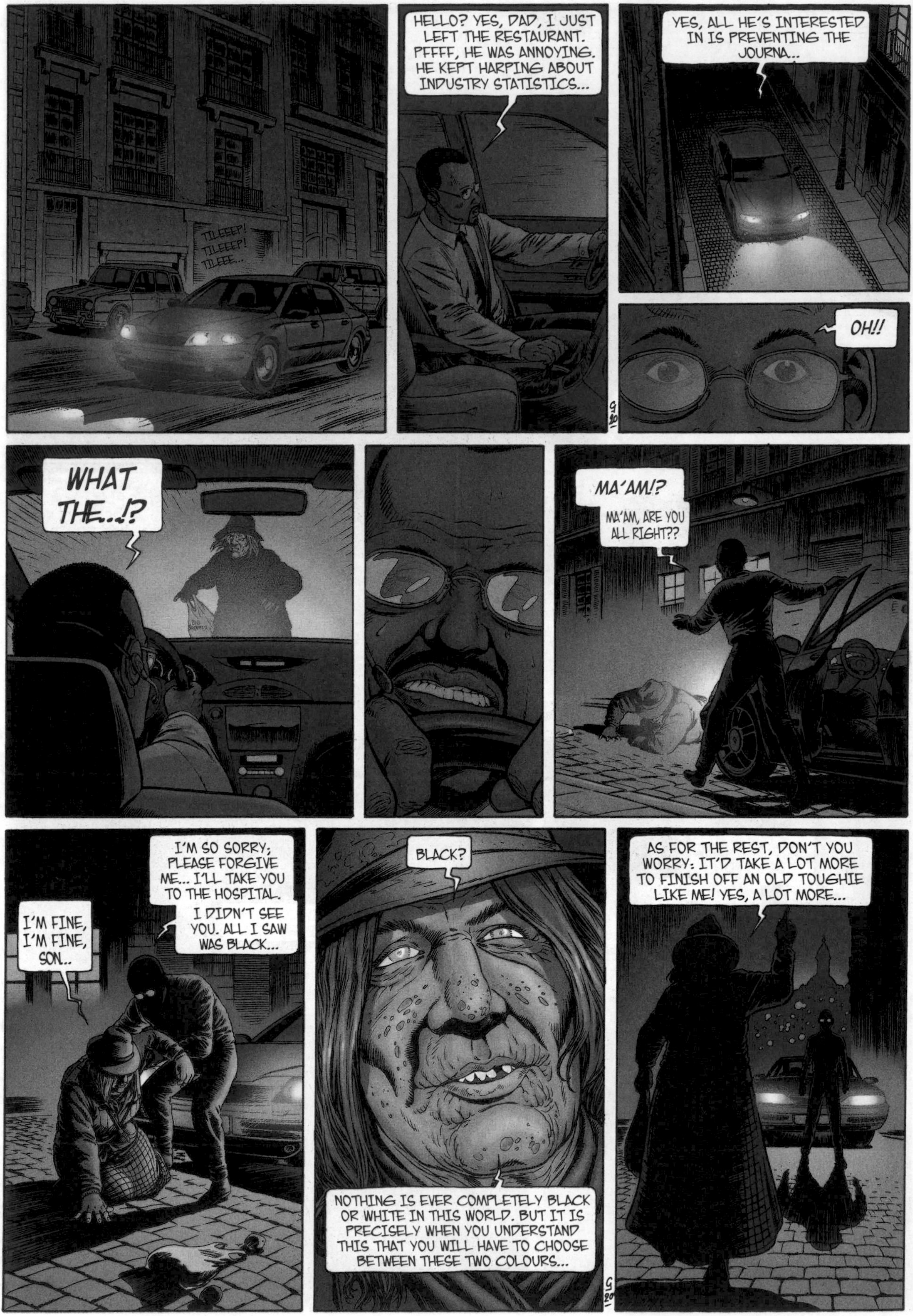
TILEEEP! TILEEEP! TILEEE...
HELLO? YES, DAD, I JUST LEFT THE RESTAURANT. PFFFF, HE WAS ANNOYING. HE KEPT HARPING ABOUT INDUSTRY STATISTICS...
YES, ALL HE'S INTERESTED IN IS PREVENTING THE JOURNA...
OH!!
WHAT THE..!?
MA'AM!?
MA'AM, ARE YOU ALL RIGHT??
I'M SO SORRY; PLEASE FORGIVE ME... I'LL TAKE YOU TO THE HOSPITAL.
I DIDN'T SEE YOU. ALL I SAW WAS BLACK...
I'M FINE, I'M FINE, SON..
BLACK?
NOTHING IS EVER COMPLETELY BLACK OR WHITE IN THIS WORLD. BUT IT IS PRECISELY WHEN YOU UNDERSTAND THIS THAT YOU WILL HAVE TO CHOOSE BETWEEN THESE TWO COLOURS...
AS FOR THE REST, DON'T YOU WORRY: IT'D TAKE A LOT MORE TO FINISH OFF AN OLD TOUGHIE LIKE ME! YES, A LOT MORE...

JULY 26

WHAT EXACTLY IS THIS?!

LOOKS LIKE A NEWSPAPER.

Disturbing increase in the umber of BSE clinical tests

ealth Ministry is taking the situation
very seriously
would allow

EVER HEARD OF FREEDOM OF THE PRESS? SOME JOURNALISTS NOTICED THE INCREASE IN TESTS FROM THE AFSSA WEBSITE AND REQUESTED AN INTERVIEW WITH ME. I GRANTED IT, THAT'S ALL...

HOW IRRESPONSIBLE OF YOU! BELIEVE ME, YOU WON'T GET AWAY WITH IT! WHEN YOU ATTACK ME...

I STRIKE BACK!

AND SO THERE IS ABSOLUTELY NO REASON TO WORRY!

AND NOW I'VE COMPLETED MY PRESENTATION. LADIES AND GENTLEMEN OF THE PRESS, IF YOU HAVE ANY QUESTIONS, PLEASE...

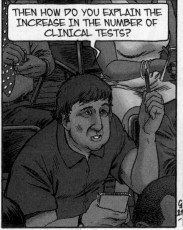

THEN HOW DO YOU EXPLAIN THE INCREASE IN THE NUMBER OF CLINICAL TESTS?

WELL, THERE CAN BE SEVERAL REASONS FOR THAT. THE HIGH TEMPERATURES WE'VE HAD COULD HAVE LOWERED THE VITAMIN B CONTENT OF THE FORAGE...

23

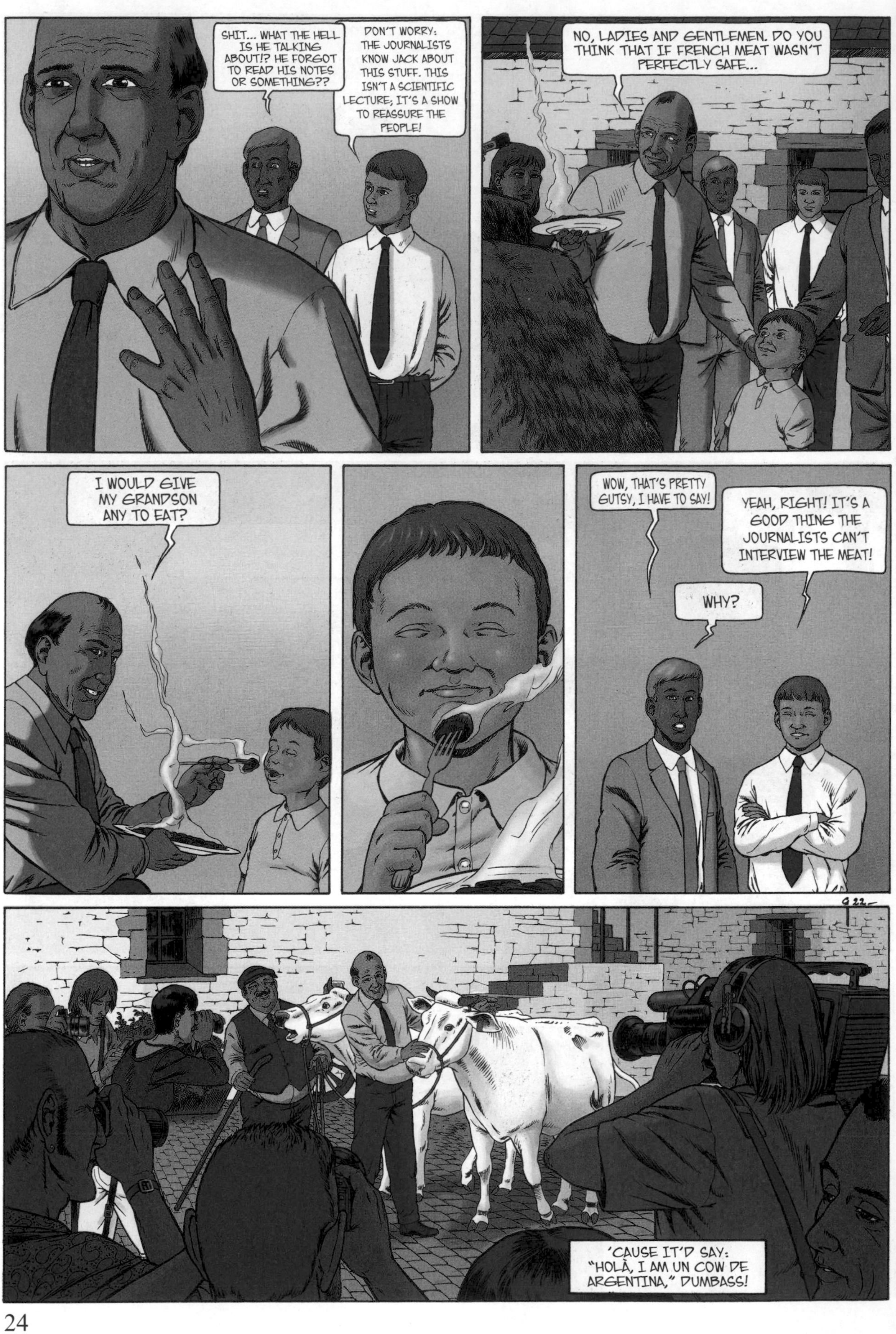
SHIT... WHAT THE HELL IS HE TALKING ABOUT!? HE FORGOT TO READ HIS NOTES OR SOMETHING??
DON'T WORRY: THE JOURNALISTS KNOW JACK ABOUT THIS STUFF. THIS ISN'T A SCIENTIFIC LECTURE; IT'S A SHOW TO REASSURE THE PEOPLE!
NO, LADIES AND GENTLEMEN. DO YOU THINK THAT IF FRENCH MEAT WASN'T PERFECTLY SAFE...
I WOULD GIVE MY GRANDSON ANY TO EAT?
WOW, THAT'S PRETTY GUTSY, I HAVE TO SAY!
YEAH, RIGHT! IT'S A GOOD THING THE JOURNALISTS CAN'T INTERVIEW THE MEAT!
WHY?
'CAUSE IT'D SAY: "HOLÀ, I AM UN COW DE ARGENTINA," DUMBASS!

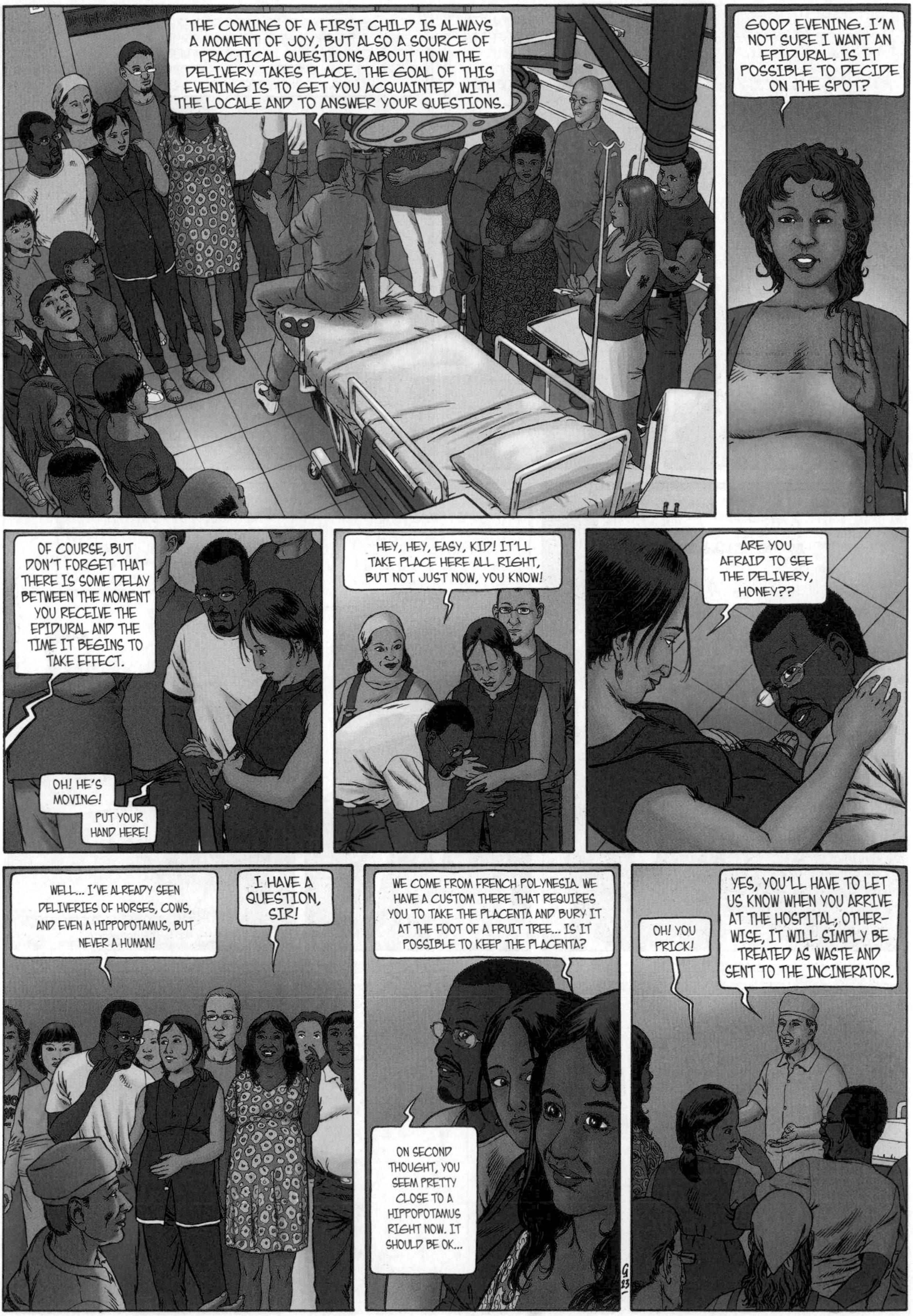
THE COMING OF A FIRST CHILD IS ALWAYS A MOMENT OF JOY, BUT ALSO A SOURCE OF PRACTICAL QUESTIONS ABOUT HOW THE DELIVERY TAKES PLACE. THE GOAL OF THIS EVENING IS TO GET YOU ACQUAINTED WITH THE LOCALE AND TO ANSWER YOUR QUESTIONS.
GOOD EVENING. I'M NOT SURE I WANT AN EPIDURAL. IS IT POSSIBLE TO DECIDE ON THE SPOT?
OF COURSE, BUT DON'T FORGET THAT THERE IS SOME DELAY BETWEEN THE MOMENT YOU RECEIVE THE EPIDURAL AND THE TIME IT BEGINS TO TAKE EFFECT.
OH! HE'S MOVING!
PUT YOUR HAND HERE!
HEY, HEY, EASY, KID! IT'LL TAKE PLACE HERE ALL RIGHT, BUT NOT JUST NOW, YOU KNOW!
ARE YOU AFRAID TO SEE THE DELIVERY, HONEY??
WELL... I'VE ALREADY SEEN DELIVERIES OF HORSES, COWS, AND EVEN A HIPPOPOTAMUS, BUT NEVER A HUMAN!
I HAVE A QUESTION, SIR!
WE COME FROM FRENCH POLYNESIA. WE HAVE A CUSTOM THERE THAT REQUIRES YOU TO TAKE THE PLACENTA AND BURY IT AT THE FOOT OF A FRUIT TREE... IS IT POSSIBLE TO KEEP THE PLACENTA?
ON SECOND THOUGHT, YOU SEEM PRETTY CLOSE TO A HIPPOPOTAMUS RIGHT NOW. IT SHOULD BE OK...
OH! YOU PRICK!
YES, YOU'LL HAVE TO LET US KNOW WHEN YOU ARRIVE AT THE HOSPITAL; OTHERWISE, IT WILL SIMPLY BE TREATED AS WASTE AND SENT TO THE INCINERATOR.

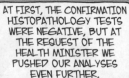

PLEASE REPEAT THIS FOR ME SLOWLY, MISS.

AT FIRST, THE CONFIRMATION HISTOPATHOLOGY TESTS WERE NEGATIVE, BUT AT THE REQUEST OF THE HEALTH MINISTER WE PUSHED OUR ANALYSES EVEN FURTHER.

USUALLY, TESTING IS FOCUSED ON A SPECIFIC PART OF THE BRAIN—THE CEREBRAL TRUNK. WE DIDN'T FIND ANYTHING IN THERE. HOWEVER, ELSE-WHERE, IN THE CEREBELLUM, WE HAVE OBSERVED LESIONS CHARACTERISTIC OF TSSE[1]!

IN OTHER WORDS: WE ARE, IN FACT, DEALING WITH A PRION[2]-BASED DISEASE. EVEN IF IT SEEMS TO HAVE TAKEN A NEW FORM, AS IT IS UNDETECTABLE BY THE USUAL TESTS! THIS IS EXTREMELY TROUBLING...

WAIT A MINUTE! EVEN IF WE ADMIT THAT THIS NASTY BUGGER FOUND ITS WAY INTO THE BRAIN OF A VERY SMALL NUMBER OF COWS...

WE HAD 80 REQUESTED TESTS IN JULY. EIGHT TIMES MORE THAN USUAL! THE EVOLUTION IS EXPONENTIAL...

DON'T INTERRUPT ME! YOU'RE FORGETTING THAT THE SRM[3] DON'T ENTER INTO HUMAN CONSUMPTION! THEY'RE ALL REMOVED IN THE SLAUGHTERHOUSES! THERE'S ZERO RISK TO HUMANS!

AND IF WE WANT EXTRA SAFETY, WE COULD SYSTEMATIZE THIS TEST AT THE SLAUGHTERHOUSE AND COMPLETELY REMOVE THOSE ANIMALS THAT MIGHT TEST POSITIVE.

IN ITS CURRENT CONFIGURATION, THAT'S OUT OF THE QUESTION. IT'S MUCH TOO EXPENSIVE AND THE RESULTS ARE TOO SLOW TO ARRIVE!

I GAVE INSTRUCTIONS THAT A NEW TEST BE DEVELOPED, ANTE MORTEM[4] IF POSSIBLE.

BUT IN THE MEANTIME, WE CANNOT SIMPLY STAND IDLY BY. HEALTH IS A PRICELESS COMMODITY...

BUT IT HAS A COST, DAMMIT! AND I REFUSE TO LET IT BE DUMPED ON THE INDUSTRY AGAIN!!!

[1]TSSE: TRANSMISSIBLE SUBACUTE SPONGIFORM ENCEPHALOPATHIES, THE "FAMILY" OF DISEASES TO WHICH BSE BELONGS
[2]NAME GIVEN TO THE TRANSMISSIBLE AGENT RESPONSIBLE FOR TSSE. FOR THE MAJORITY OF EXPERTS, IT IS AN ABNORMAL FORM OF A PROTEIN THAT ACCUMULATES IN THE BRAINS OF THE VICTIMS OF TSSE.
[3]SPECIFIED RISK MATERIALS ARE THE TISSUES LIKELY TO CONTAIN PRIONS (BRAIN, EYES, SPINAL CHORD, ETC...) IN DISEASED ANIMALS.
[4]"PRIOR TO DEATH"—MEANING THAT IT CAN BE CARRIED OUT ON LIVE ANIMALS AND NOT REQUIRE THAT THEY BE SLAUGHTERED.

THIS DISEASE TURNS YOUR BRAIN INTO A SPONGE, DAMMIT! CAN YOU IMAGINE WHAT IT WOULD BE LIKE FOR A HUMAN BEING?!

BUT HOW ON EARTH DO YOU THINK THAT COULD HAPPEN, SINCE THE SRM ARE REMOVED FROM THE FOOD CHAIN?

WHAT IF THIS NEW FORM OF THE PRION COULD MOVE TO PARTS OTHER THAN THE SRM? IMAGINE IF IT COULD BE FOUND IN THE MEAT!?

NONSENSE!! WE'VE NEVER OBSERVED ANYTHING LIKE THAT IN BOVINES!

WE CANNOT REJECT THE HYPOTHESIS OUT OF HAND.

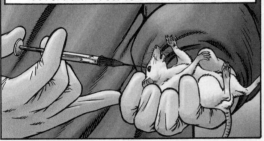

I HAD CONTAMINATED COWS' SPLEEN INJECTED INTO THE BRAINS OF LAB MICE. IT'S THE ONLY METHOD THAT CAN CONFIRM OR DISPROVE THIS HYPOTHESIS. BUT IT WILL TAKE SEVERAL MONTHS BEFORE ANY RESULTS CAN BE OBSERVED.

WELL, THEN, LET'S WAIT UNTIL WE HAVE THEM BEFORE WE MAKE COMPLETE FOOLS OF OURSELVES BY TAKING MEASURES! BECAUSE, AT THIS MINUTE, YOU HAVE ABSOLUTELY NO INDICATION THAT LEADS ME TO THINK THIS DISEASE COULD PRESENT ANY SORT OF DANGER TO HUMANS! DO YOU HEAR?

AHAHAHAHA

ABSOLUTELY NONE!

STOP IT!

OLIVIER, WHAT'S GOING ON!?

AHAHAHAHAH!

MY GOD, OLIVIER... I THINK YOU'RE LOSING YOUR MIND...

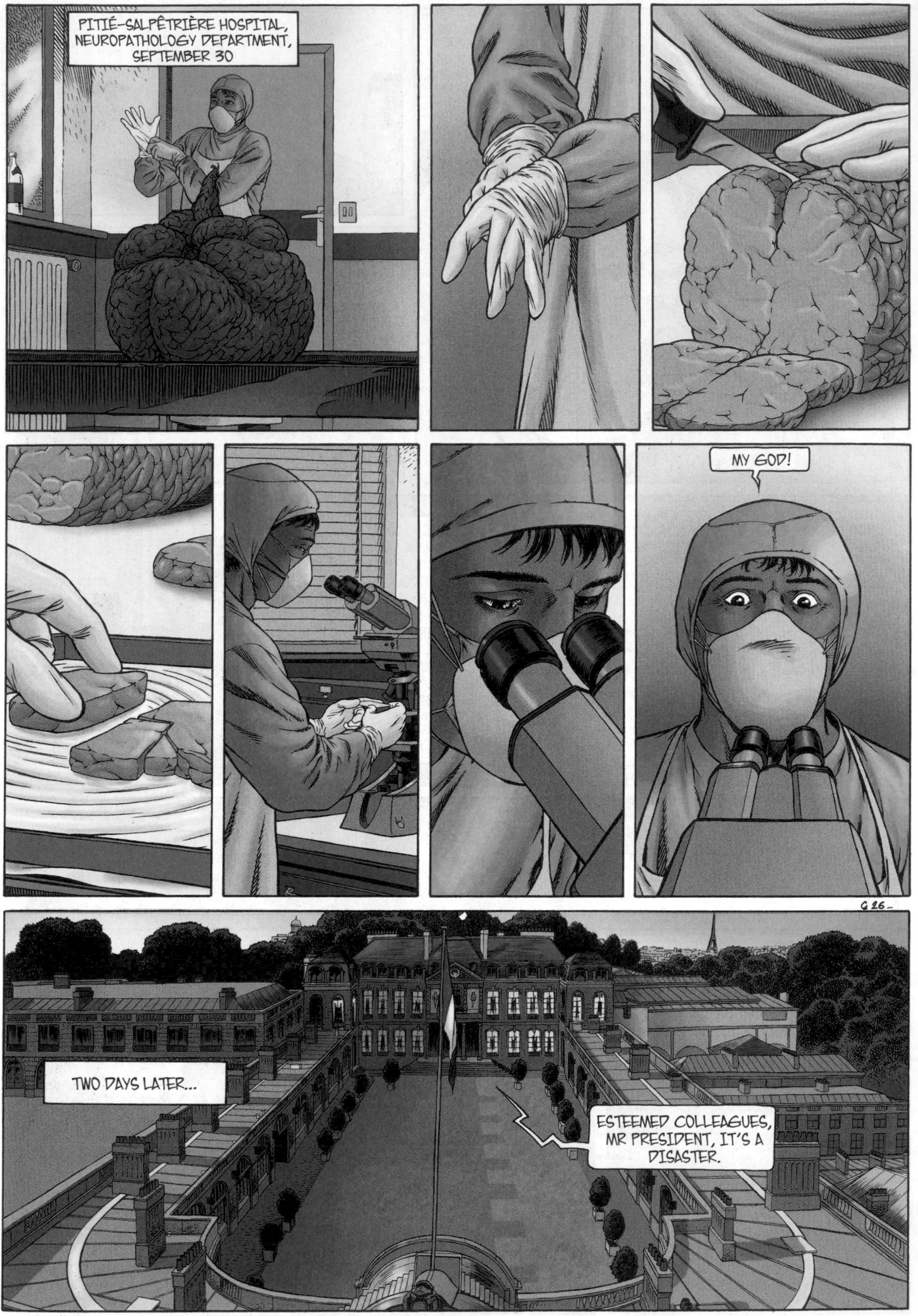
PITIÉ-SALPÊTRIÈRE HOSPITAL, NEUROPATHOLOGY DEPARTMENT, SEPTEMBER 30
MY GOD!
TWO DAYS LATER...
ESTEEMED COLLEAGUES, MR PRESIDENT, IT'S A DISASTER.

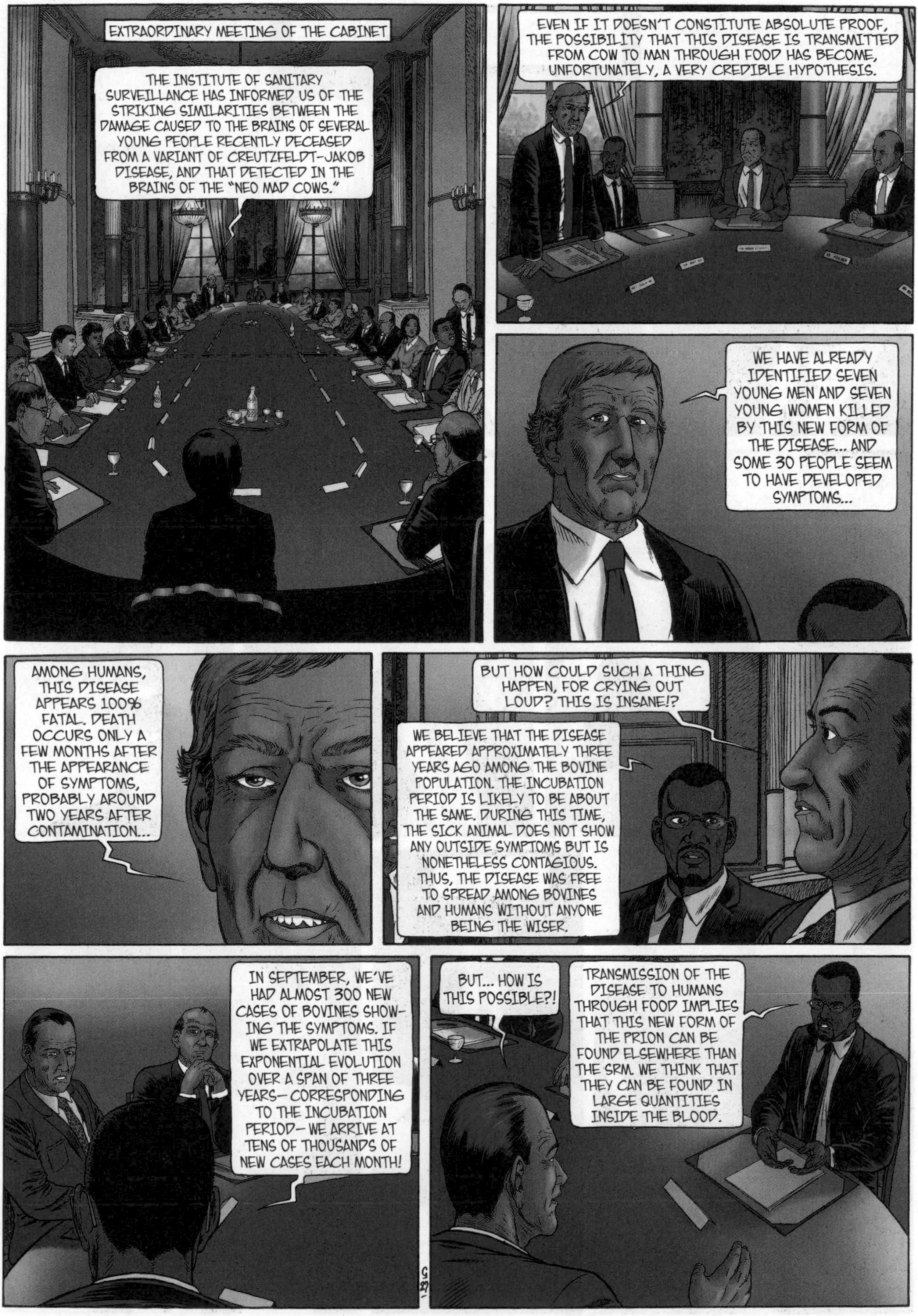
EXTRAORDINARY MEETING OF THE CABINET
THE INSTITUTE OF SANITARY SURVEILLANCE HAS INFORMED US OF THE STRIKING SIMILARITIES BETWEEN THE DAMAGE CAUSED TO THE BRAINS OF SEVERAL YOUNG PEOPLE RECENTLY DECEASED FROM A VARIANT OF CREUTZFELDT-JAKOB DISEASE, AND THAT DETECTED IN THE BRAINS OF THE "NEO MAD COWS."
EVEN IF IT DOESN'T CONSTITUTE ABSOLUTE PROOF, THE POSSIBILITY THAT THIS DISEASE IS TRANSMITTED FROM COW TO MAN THROUGH FOOD HAS BECOME, UNFORTUNATELY, A VERY CREDIBLE HYPOTHESIS.
WE HAVE ALREADY IDENTIFIED SEVEN YOUNG MEN AND SEVEN YOUNG WOMEN KILLED BY THIS NEW FORM OF THE DISEASE... AND SOME 30 PEOPLE SEEM TO HAVE DEVELOPED SYMPTOMS...
AMONG HUMANS, THIS DISEASE APPEARS 100% FATAL. DEATH OCCURS ONLY A FEW MONTHS AFTER THE APPEARANCE OF SYMPTOMS, PROBABLY AROUND TWO YEARS AFTER CONTAMINATION...
BUT HOW COULD SUCH A THING HAPPEN, FOR CRYING OUT LOUD? THIS IS INSANE!?
WE BELIEVE THAT THE DISEASE APPEARED APPROXIMATELY THREE YEARS AGO AMONG THE BOVINE POPULATION. THE INCUBATION PERIOD IS LIKELY TO BE ABOUT THE SAME. DURING THIS TIME, THE SICK ANIMAL DOES NOT SHOW ANY OUTSIDE SYMPTOMS BUT IS NONETHELESS CONTAGIOUS. THUS, THE DISEASE WAS FREE TO SPREAD AMONG BOVINES AND HUMANS WITHOUT ANYONE BEING THE WISER.
IN SEPTEMBER, WE'VE HAD ALMOST 300 NEW CASES OF BOVINES SHOWING THE SYMPTOMS. IF WE EXTRAPOLATE THIS EXPONENTIAL EVOLUTION OVER A SPAN OF THREE YEARS— CORRESPONDING TO THE INCUBATION PERIOD— WE ARRIVE AT TENS OF THOUSANDS OF NEW CASES EACH MONTH!
BUT... HOW IS THIS POSSIBLE?!
TRANSMISSION OF THE DISEASE TO HUMANS THROUGH FOOD IMPLIES THAT THIS NEW FORM OF THE PRION CAN BE FOUND ELSEWHERE THAN THE SRM. WE THINK THAT THEY CAN BE FOUND IN LARGE QUANTITIES INSIDE THE BLOOD.

IF THERE ARE PRIONS IN THE BLOODSTREAM, THEY WILL ALSO BE FOUND IN MILK, EXCREMENT, SALIVA... CONTAGION WITHIN A HERD WILL BE QUICK.

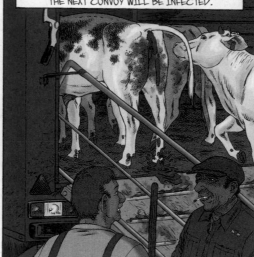

SIMILARLY, IF A TRUCK TRANSPORTING CONTAMINATED ANIMALS IS INSUFFICIENTLY DISINFECTED, THE NEXT CONVOY WILL BE INFECTED.

TRANSMISSION CAN ALSO COME FROM A VETERINARY SURGEON VISITING DIFFERENT FARMS, OR DURING CATTLE FAIRS, ETC, ETC. IT'S A LONG LIST.

LITTLE BY LITTLE, SINCE THE BSE TEST COULD NOT DETECT THEM, DISEASED ANIMALS THAT HADN'T YET DEVELOPED SYMPTOMS PENETRATED THE HUMAN FOOD CHAIN...

DO WE HAVE ANY IDEA OF THE NUMBER OF SICK ANIMALS THAT COULD HAVE ENTERED THE FOOD CHAIN?

AT THIS STAGE, WE CAN ONLY ESTI...

HOW MANY?!?

IN ALL LIKELIHOOD, SEVERAL HUNDRED THOUSAND, MR PRESIDENT... WE CAN EXPECT HUNDREDS OF HUMAN VICTIMS...

... MINIMUM.

THIS IS A NIGHTMARE...

BUT WHAT CAN EXPLAIN THIS NEW DISEASE? DAMMIT, WHERE DOES IT COME FROM?

TO TELL YOU THE TRUTH, MR PRESIDENT...

... I DON'T HAVE THE SLIGHTEST IDEA...

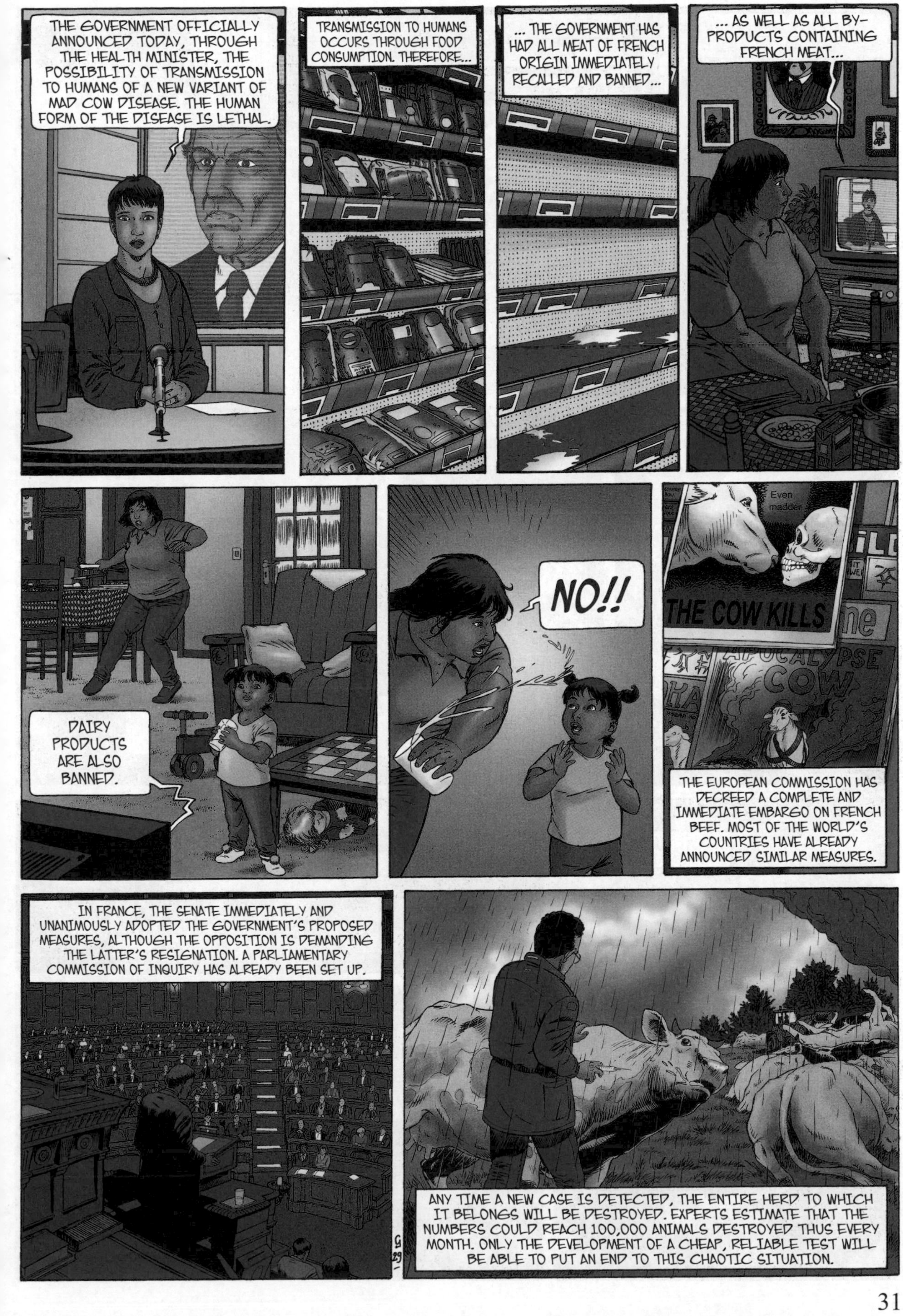
THE GOVERNMENT OFFICIALLY ANNOUNCED TODAY, THROUGH THE HEALTH MINISTER, THE POSSIBILITY OF TRANSMISSION TO HUMANS OF A NEW VARIANT OF MAD COW DISEASE. THE HUMAN FORM OF THE DISEASE IS LETHAL.
TRANSMISSION TO HUMANS OCCURS THROUGH FOOD CONSUMPTION. THEREFORE...
... THE GOVERNMENT HAS HAD ALL MEAT OF FRENCH ORIGIN IMMEDIATELY RECALLED AND BANNED...
... AS WELL AS ALL BY-PRODUCTS CONTAINING FRENCH MEAT...
DAIRY PRODUCTS ARE ALSO BANNED.
NO!!
Even madder
THE COW KILLS
APOCALYPSE COW
THE EUROPEAN COMMISSION HAS DECREED A COMPLETE AND IMMEDIATE EMBARGO ON FRENCH BEEF. MOST OF THE WORLD'S COUNTRIES HAVE ALREADY ANNOUNCED SIMILAR MEASURES.
IN FRANCE, THE SENATE IMMEDIATELY AND UNANIMOUSLY ADOPTED THE GOVERNMENT'S PROPOSED MEASURES, ALTHOUGH THE OPPOSITION IS DEMANDING THE LATTER'S RESIGNATION. A PARLIAMENTARY COMMISSION OF INQUIRY HAS ALREADY BEEN SET UP.
ANY TIME A NEW CASE IS DETECTED, THE ENTIRE HERD TO WHICH IT BELONGS WILL BE DESTROYED. EXPERTS ESTIMATE THAT THE NUMBERS COULD REACH 100,000 ANIMALS DESTROYED THUS EVERY MONTH. ONLY THE DEVELOPMENT OF A CHEAP, RELIABLE TEST WILL BE ABLE TO PUT AN END TO THIS CHAOTIC SITUATION.

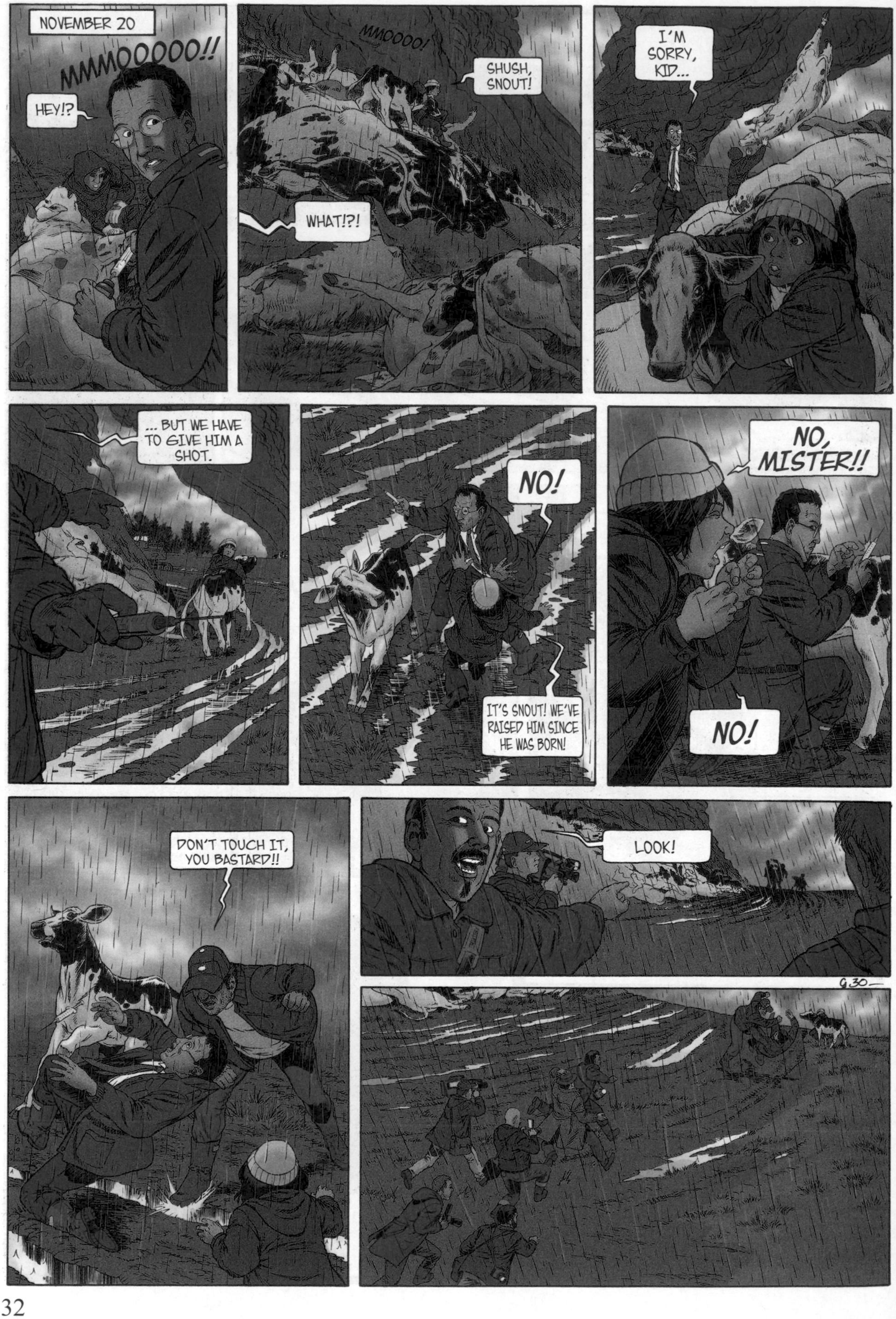
NOVEMBER 20
MMMOOOOO!!
HEY!?
MMOOOO!
SHUSH, SNOUT!
WHAT!?!
I'M SORRY, KID...
... BUT WE HAVE TO GIVE HIM A SHOT.
NO!
IT'S SNOUT! WE'VE RAISED HIM SINCE HE WAS BORN!
NO, MISTER!!
NO!
DON'T TOUCH IT, YOU BASTARD!!
LOOK!

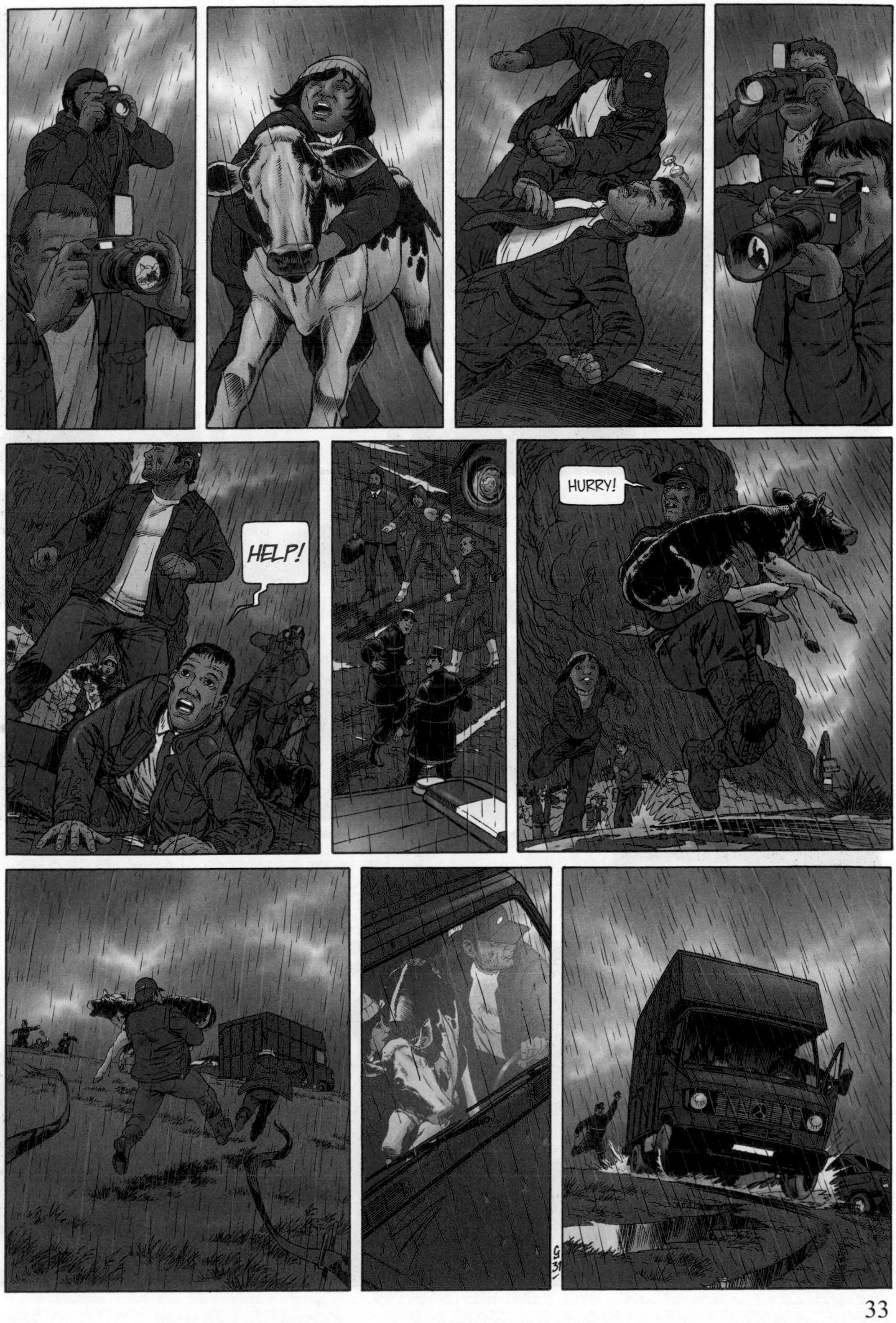
HELP!
HURRY!

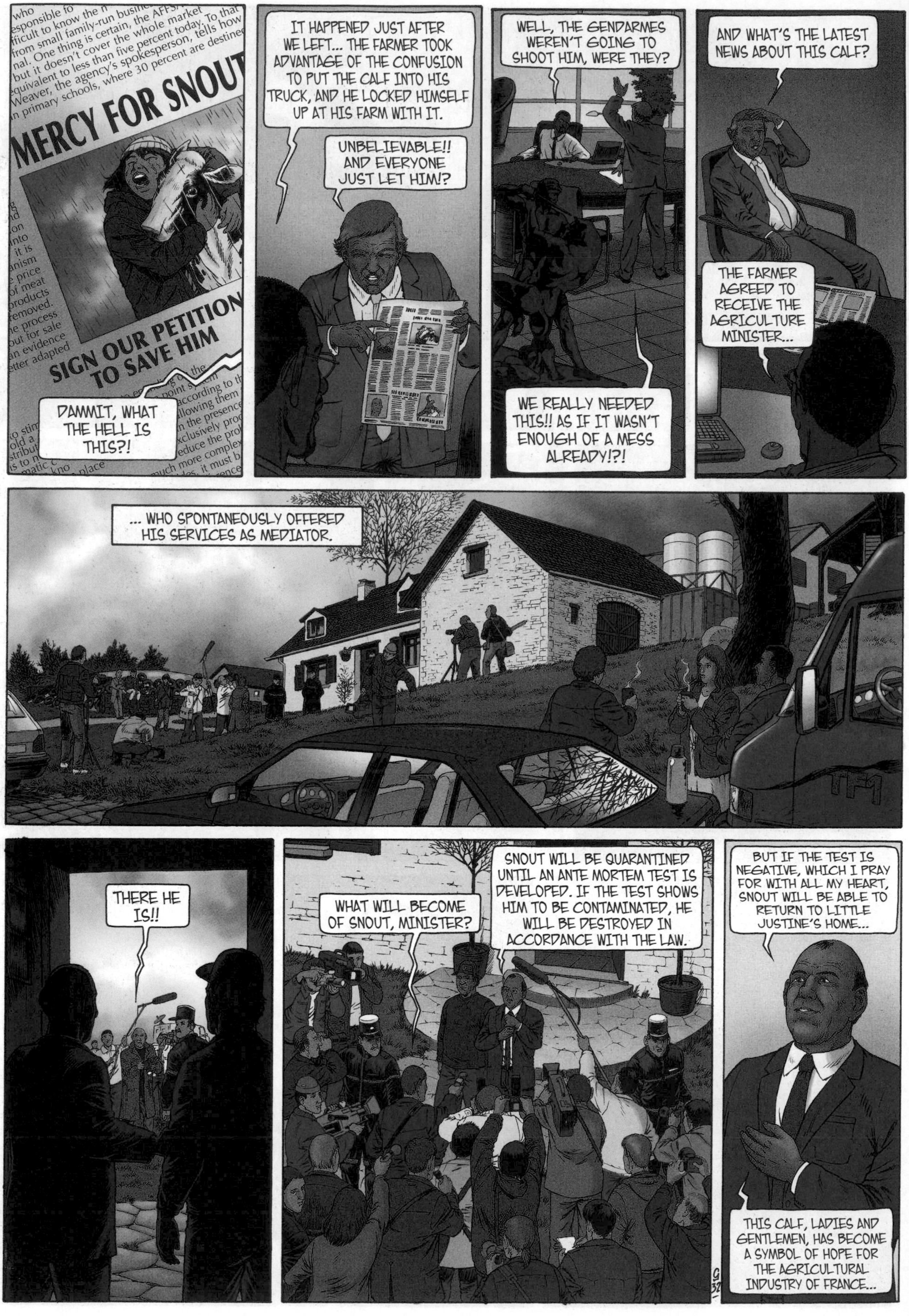
MERCY FOR SNOUT
SIGN OUR PETITION TO SAVE HIM
DAMMIT, WHAT THE HELL IS THIS?!
IT HAPPENED JUST AFTER WE LEFT... THE FARMER TOOK ADVANTAGE OF THE CONFUSION TO PUT THE CALF INTO HIS TRUCK, AND HE LOCKED HIMSELF UP AT HIS FARM WITH IT.
UNBELIEVABLE!! AND EVERYONE JUST LET HIM!?
WELL, THE GENDARMES WEREN'T GOING TO SHOOT HIM, WERE THEY?
WE REALLY NEEDED THIS!! AS IF IT WASN'T ENOUGH OF A MESS ALREADY!?!
AND WHAT'S THE LATEST NEWS ABOUT THIS CALF?
THE FARMER AGREED TO RECEIVE THE AGRICULTURE MINISTER...
... WHO SPONTANEOUSLY OFFERED HIS SERVICES AS MEDIATOR.
THERE HE IS!!
WHAT WILL BECOME OF SNOUT, MINISTER?
SNOUT WILL BE QUARANTINED UNTIL AN ANTE MORTEM TEST IS DEVELOPED. IF THE TEST SHOWS HIM TO BE CONTAMINATED, HE WILL BE DESTROYED IN ACCORDANCE WITH THE LAW.
BUT IF THE TEST IS NEGATIVE, WHICH I PRAY FOR WITH ALL MY HEART, SNOUT WILL BE ABLE TO RETURN TO LITTLE JUSTINE'S HOME...
THIS CALF, LADIES AND GENTLEMEN, HAS BECOME A SYMBOL OF HOPE FOR THE AGRICULTURAL INDUSTRY OF FRANCE...

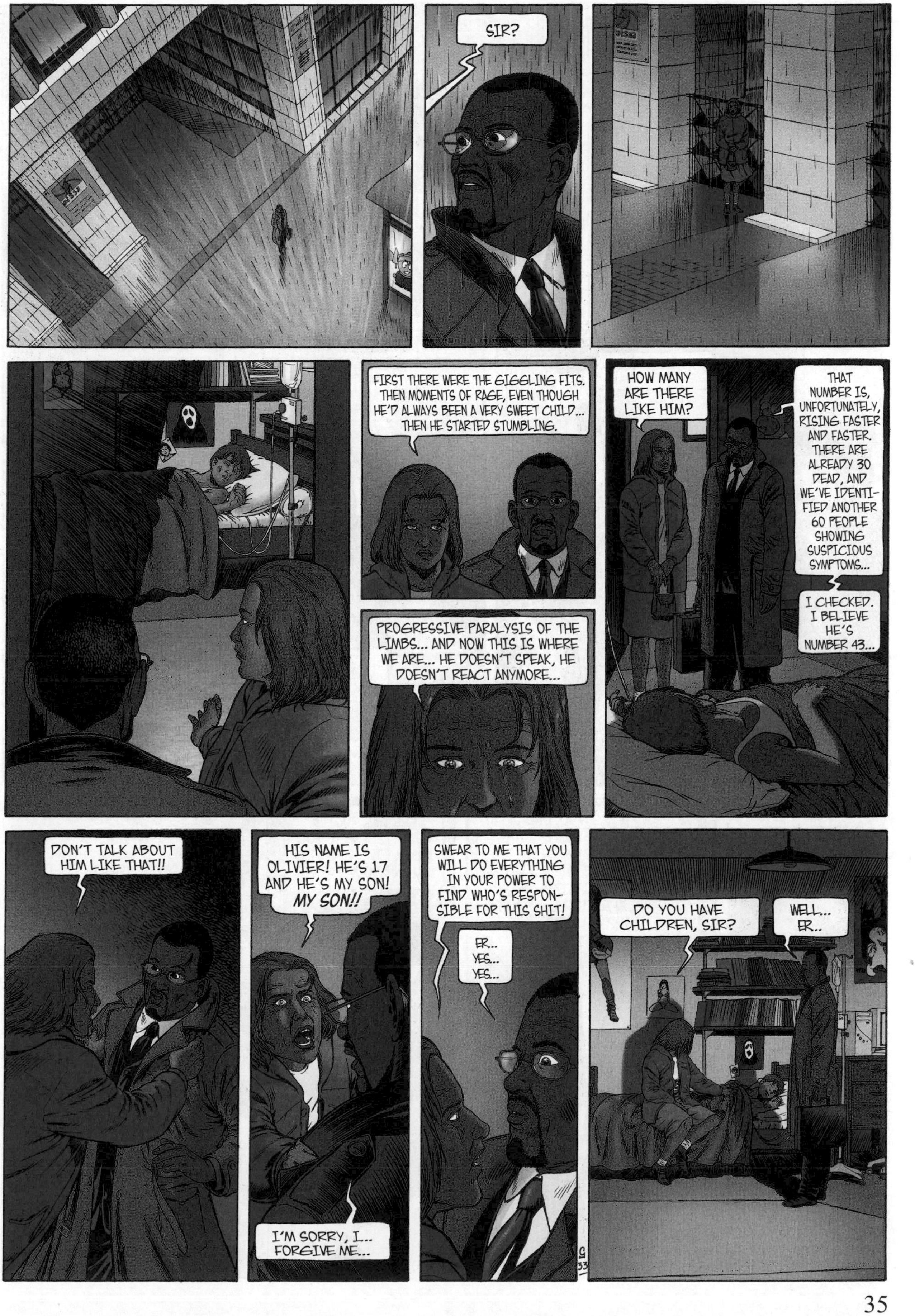

SIR?
FIRST THERE WERE THE GIGGLING FITS. THEN MOMENTS OF RAGE, EVEN THOUGH HE'D ALWAYS BEEN A VERY SWEET CHILD... THEN HE STARTED STUMBLING.
PROGRESSIVE PARALYSIS OF THE LIMBS... AND NOW THIS IS WHERE WE ARE... HE DOESN'T SPEAK, HE DOESN'T REACT ANYMORE...
HOW MANY ARE THERE LIKE HIM?
THAT NUMBER IS, UNFORTUNATELY, RISING FASTER AND FASTER. THERE ARE ALREADY 30 DEAD, AND WE'VE IDENTIFIED ANOTHER 60 PEOPLE SHOWING SUSPICIOUS SYMPTOMS...
I CHECKED. I BELIEVE HE'S NUMBER 43...
DON'T TALK ABOUT HIM LIKE THAT!!
HIS NAME IS OLIVIER! HE'S 17 AND HE'S MY SON! MY SON!!
I'M SORRY, I... FORGIVE ME...
SWEAR TO ME THAT YOU WILL DO EVERYTHING IN YOUR POWER TO FIND WHO'S RESPONSIBLE FOR THIS SHIT!
ER.. YES... YES...
DO YOU HAVE CHILDREN, SIR?
WELL... ER..

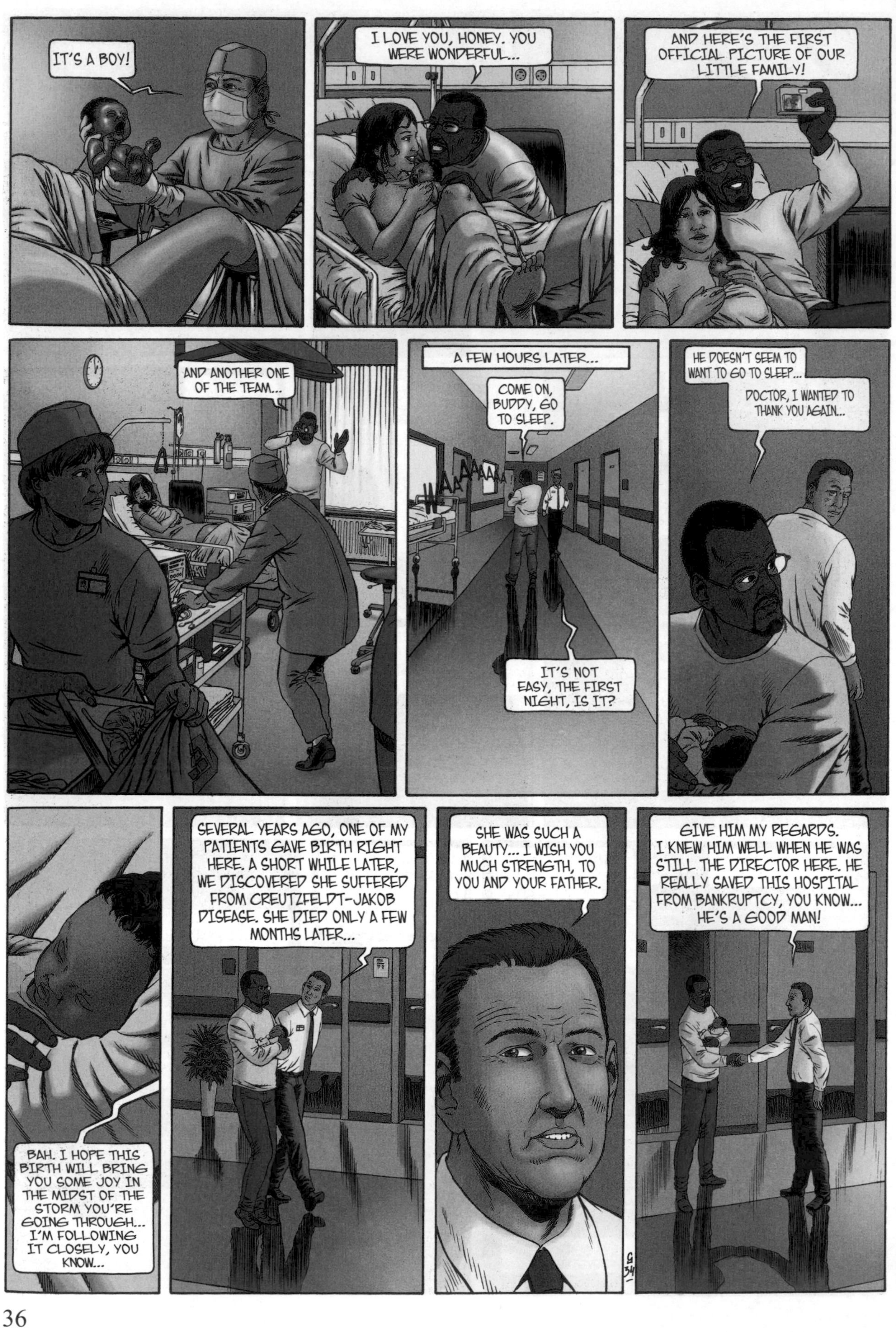
IT'S A BOY!
I LOVE YOU, HONEY. YOU WERE WONDERFUL...
AND HERE'S THE FIRST OFFICIAL PICTURE OF OUR LITTLE FAMILY!
AND ANOTHER ONE OF THE TEAM...
A FEW HOURS LATER...
COME ON, BUDDY, GO TO SLEEP.
IT'S NOT EASY, THE FIRST NIGHT, IS IT?
HE DOESN'T SEEM TO WANT TO GO TO SLEEP...
DOCTOR, I WANTED TO THANK YOU AGAIN...
BAH. I HOPE THIS BIRTH WILL BRING YOU SOME JOY IN THE MIDST OF THE STORM YOU'RE GOING THROUGH... I'M FOLLOWING IT CLOSELY, YOU KNOW...
SEVERAL YEARS AGO, ONE OF MY PATIENTS GAVE BIRTH RIGHT HERE. A SHORT WHILE LATER, WE DISCOVERED SHE SUFFERED FROM CREUTZFELDT-JAKOB DISEASE. SHE DIED ONLY A FEW MONTHS LATER...
SHE WAS SUCH A BEAUTY... I WISH YOU MUCH STRENGTH, TO YOU AND YOUR FATHER.
GIVE HIM MY REGARDS. I KNEW HIM WELL WHEN HE WAS STILL THE DIRECTOR HERE. HE REALLY SAVED THIS HOSPITAL FROM BANKRUPTCY, YOU KNOW... HE'S A GOOD MAN!

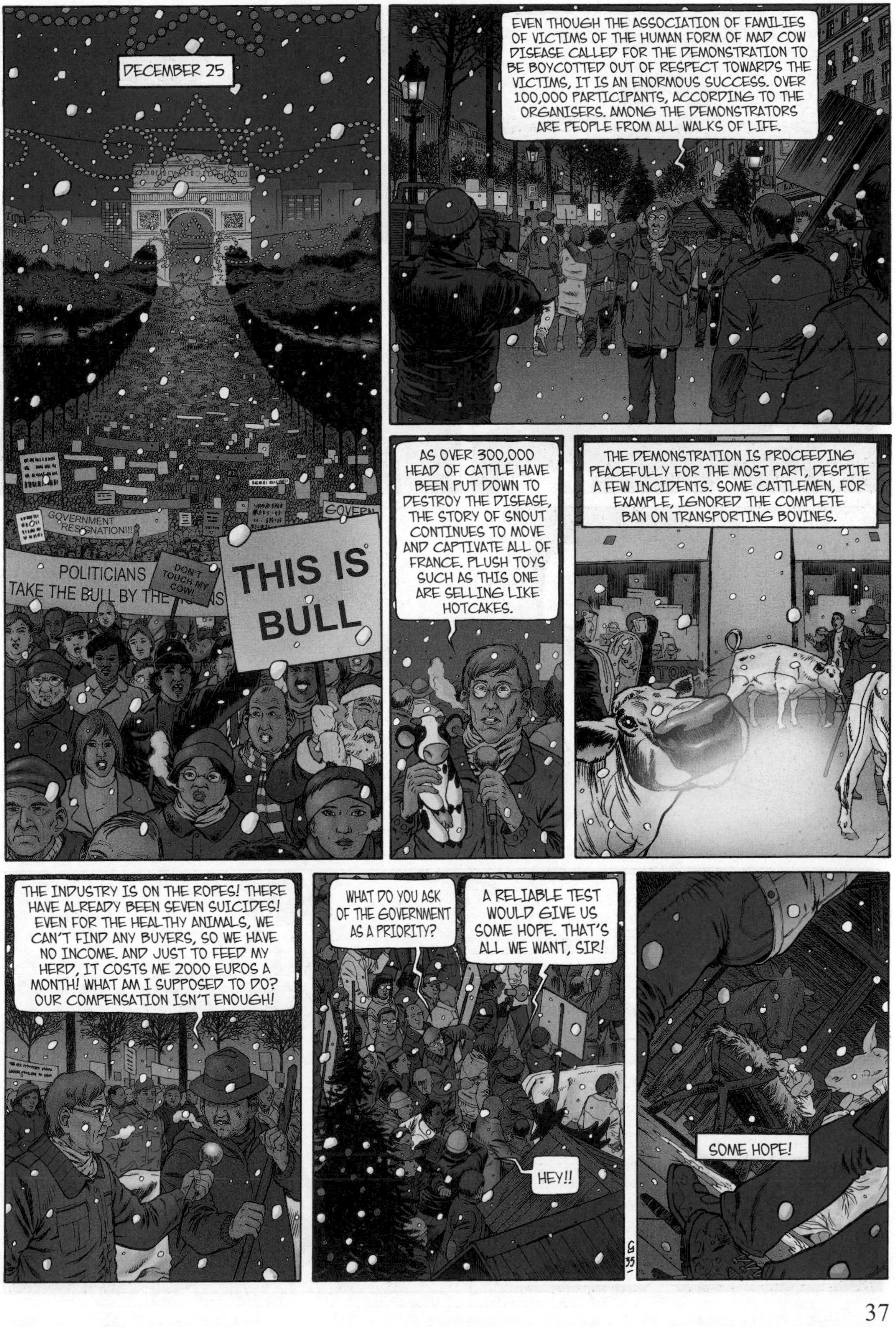
DECEMBER 25
GOVERNMENT RESIGNATION!!!
POLITICIANS TAKE THE BULL BY THE
DON'T TOUCH MY COW!
THIS IS BULL
EVEN THOUGH THE ASSOCIATION OF FAMILIES OF VICTIMS OF THE HUMAN FORM OF MAD COW DISEASE CALLED FOR THE DEMONSTRATION TO BE BOYCOTTED OUT OF RESPECT TOWARDS THE VICTIMS, IT IS AN ENORMOUS SUCCESS. OVER 100,000 PARTICIPANTS, ACCORDING TO THE ORGANISERS. AMONG THE DEMONSTRATORS ARE PEOPLE FROM ALL WALKS OF LIFE.
AS OVER 300,000 HEAD OF CATTLE HAVE BEEN PUT DOWN TO DESTROY THE DISEASE, THE STORY OF SNOUT CONTINUES TO MOVE AND CAPTIVATE ALL OF FRANCE. PLUSH TOYS SUCH AS THIS ONE ARE SELLING LIKE HOTCAKES.
THE DEMONSTRATION IS PROCEEDING PEACEFULLY FOR THE MOST PART, DESPITE A FEW INCIDENTS. SOME CATTLEMEN, FOR EXAMPLE, IGNORED THE COMPLETE BAN ON TRANSPORTING BOVINES.
THE INDUSTRY IS ON THE ROPES! THERE HAVE ALREADY BEEN SEVEN SUICIDES! EVEN FOR THE HEALTHY ANIMALS, WE CAN'T FIND ANY BUYERS, SO WE HAVE NO INCOME. AND JUST TO FEED MY HERD, IT COSTS ME 2000 EUROS A MONTH! WHAT AM I SUPPOSED TO DO? OUR COMPENSATION ISN'T ENOUGH!
WHAT DO YOU ASK OF THE GOVERNMENT AS A PRIORITY?
A RELIABLE TEST WOULD GIVE US SOME HOPE. THAT'S ALL WE WANT, SIR!
HEY!!
SOME HOPE!

THIS IS THE CONCLUSION WE'VE REACHED.

CASES OF CONTAMINATED ANIMALS APPEARED GRADUALLY THROUGHOUT FRANCE, ON VARIOUS FARMS.

THEREFORE, WE THOUGHT AT FIRST THAT THE CONTAMINATING AGENT WAS MASSIVELY PRESENT IN THE COUNTRY, AS MBM WAS DURING THE FIRST MAD COW CRISIS.

BUT NO COMMONALITY COULD BE ESTABLISHED AMONG THESE VARIOUS FARMS, WHETHER IN THE ANIMAL FEED OR IN THE DRUGS USED.

SO WE THEN PROCEEDED ALONG A DIFFERENT PREMISE. WE FIGURED THAT A VERY SMALL NUMBER OF ANIMALS, MAYBE A SINGLE HERD, HAD COME INTO CONTACT WITH THE CONTAMINANT. IT'S THE EXTREMELY HIGH CONTAGIOUSNESS OF THE DISEASE THAT WOULD THEN EXPLAIN ITS PROPAGATION, AND NOT A MASSIVE PRESENCE OF THE CONTAMINATING AGENT.

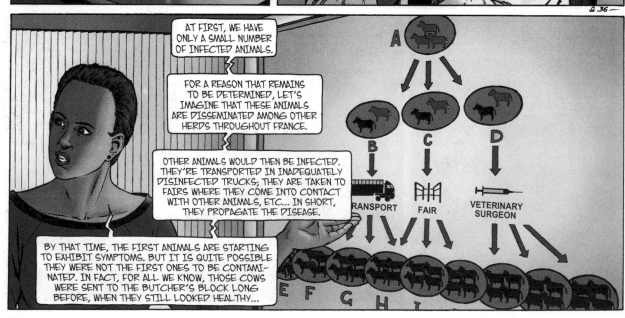

AT FIRST, WE HAVE ONLY A SMALL NUMBER OF INFECTED ANIMALS.

FOR A REASON THAT REMAINS TO BE DETERMINED, LET'S IMAGINE THAT THESE ANIMALS ARE DISSEMINATED AMONG OTHER HERDS THROUGHOUT FRANCE.

OTHER ANIMALS WOULD THEN BE INFECTED. THEY'RE TRANSPORTED IN INADEQUATELY DISINFECTED TRUCKS; THEY ARE TAKEN TO FAIRS WHERE THEY COME INTO CONTACT WITH OTHER ANIMALS, ETC... IN SHORT, THEY PROPAGATE THE DISEASE.

BY THAT TIME, THE FIRST ANIMALS ARE STARTING TO EXHIBIT SYMPTOMS. BUT IT IS QUITE POSSIBLE THEY WERE NOT THE FIRST ONES TO BE CONTAMINATED. IN FACT, FOR ALL WE KNOW, THOSE COWS WERE SENT TO THE BUTCHER'S BLOCK LONG BEFORE, WHEN THEY STILL LOOKED HEALTHY...

A

B TRANSPORT

C FAIR

D VETERINARY SURGEON

E F G H

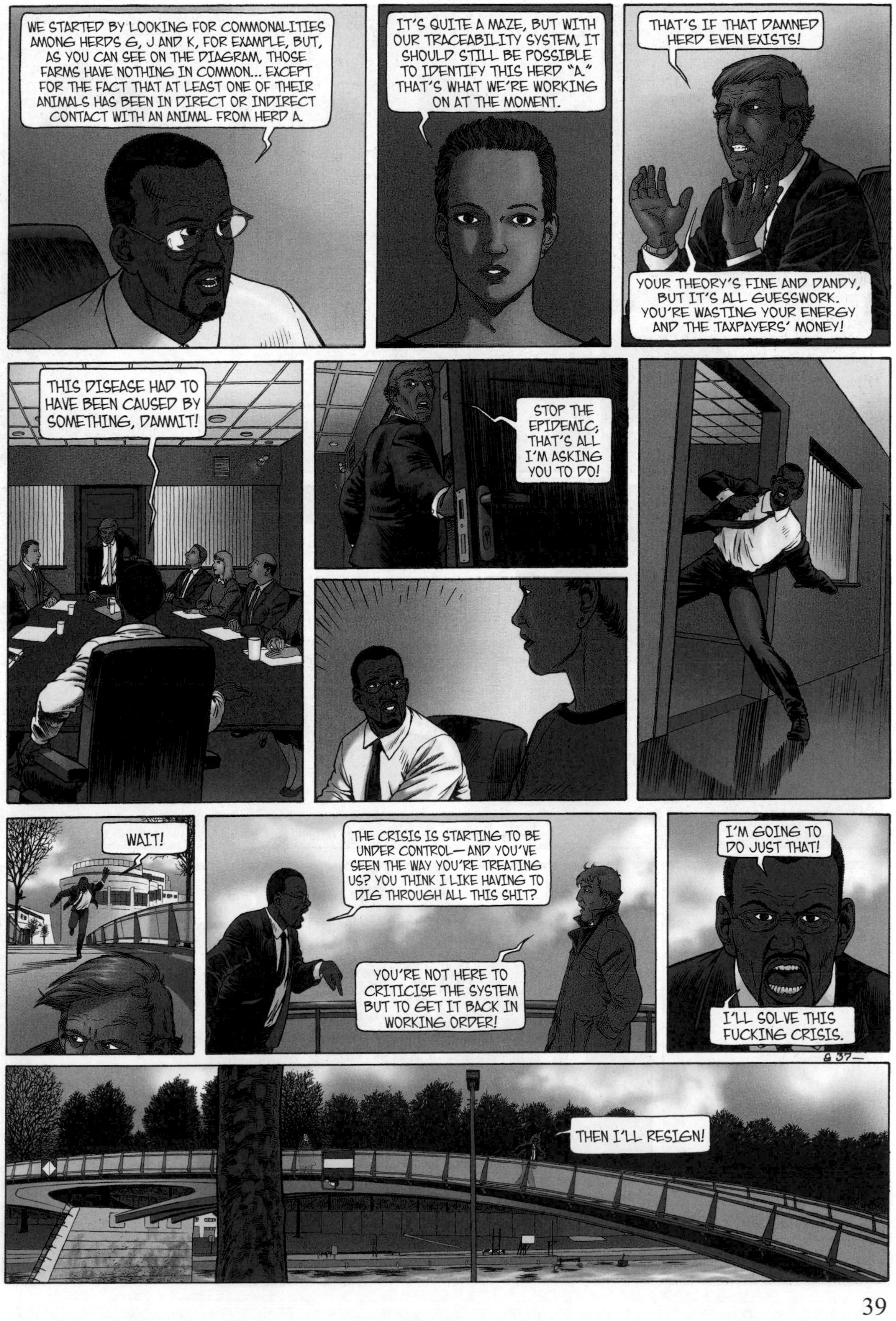
WE STARTED BY LOOKING FOR COMMONALITIES AMONG HERDS G, J AND K, FOR EXAMPLE, BUT, AS YOU CAN SEE ON THE DIAGRAM, THOSE FARMS HAVE NOTHING IN COMMON... EXCEPT FOR THE FACT THAT AT LEAST ONE OF THEIR ANIMALS HAS BEEN IN DIRECT OR INDIRECT CONTACT WITH AN ANIMAL FROM HERD A.
IT'S QUITE A MAZE, BUT WITH OUR TRACEABILITY SYSTEM, IT SHOULD STILL BE POSSIBLE TO IDENTIFY THIS HERD "A." THAT'S WHAT WE'RE WORKING ON AT THE MOMENT.
THAT'S IF THAT DAMNED HERD EVEN EXISTS!
YOUR THEORY'S FINE AND DANDY, BUT IT'S ALL GUESSWORK. YOU'RE WASTING YOUR ENERGY AND THE TAXPAYERS' MONEY!
THIS DISEASE HAD TO HAVE BEEN CAUSED BY SOMETHING, DAMMIT!
STOP THE EPIDEMIC; THAT'S ALL I'M ASKING YOU TO DO!
WAIT!
THE CRISIS IS STARTING TO BE UNDER CONTROL— AND YOU'VE SEEN THE WAY YOU'RE TREATING US? YOU THINK I LIKE HAVING TO DIG THROUGH ALL THIS SHIT?
YOU'RE NOT HERE TO CRITICISE THE SYSTEM BUT TO GET IT BACK IN WORKING ORDER!
I'M GOING TO DO JUST THAT!
I'LL SOLVE THIS FUCKING CRISIS.
THEN I'LL RESIGN!

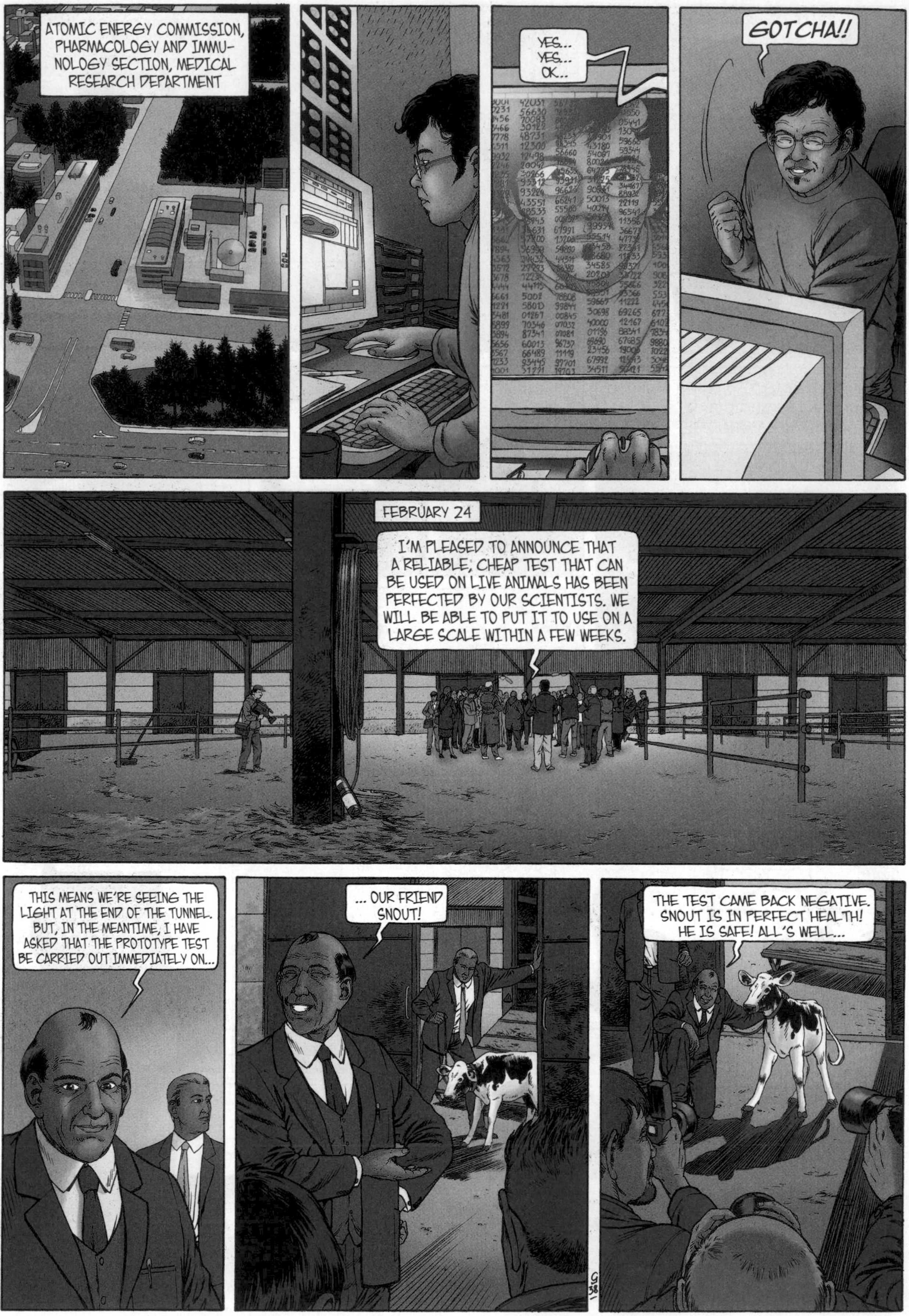
ATOMIC ENERGY COMMISSION, PHARMACOLOGY AND IMMUNOLOGY SECTION, MEDICAL RESEARCH DEPARTMENT
YES... YES... OK...
GOTCHA!!
FEBRUARY 24
I'M PLEASED TO ANNOUNCE THAT A RELIABLE, CHEAP TEST THAT CAN BE USED ON LIVE ANIMALS HAS BEEN PERFECTED BY OUR SCIENTISTS. WE WILL BE ABLE TO PUT IT TO USE ON A LARGE SCALE WITHIN A FEW WEEKS.
THIS MEANS WE'RE SEEING THE LIGHT AT THE END OF THE TUNNEL. BUT, IN THE MEANTIME, I HAVE ASKED THAT THE PROTOTYPE TEST BE CARRIED OUT IMMEDIATELY ON...
... OUR FRIEND SNOUT!
THE TEST CAME BACK NEGATIVE. SNOUT IS IN PERFECT HEALTH! HE IS SAFE! ALL'S WELL...

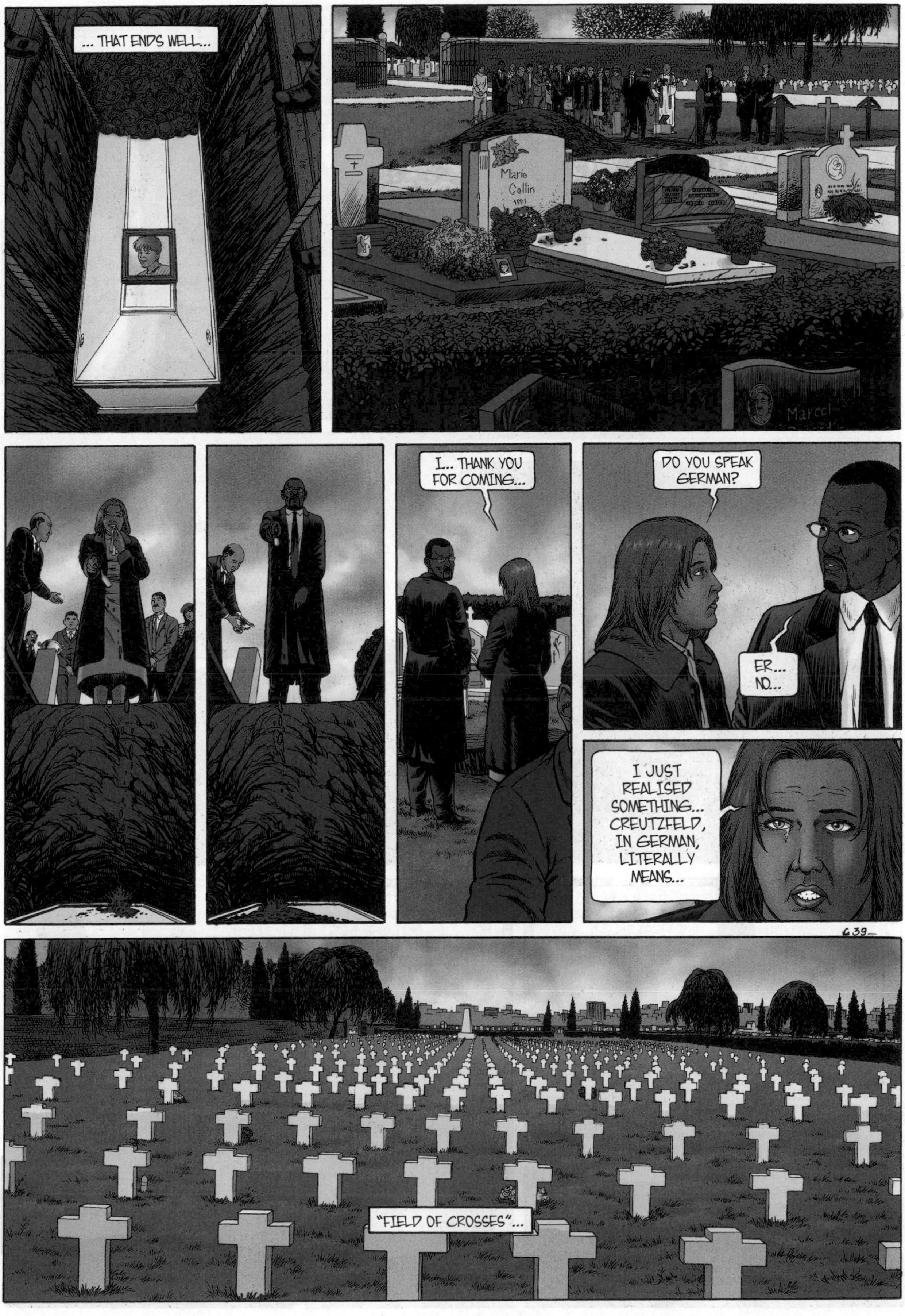
... THAT ENDS WELL...
Marie Collin
Marcel
I... THANK YOU FOR COMING...
DO YOU SPEAK GERMAN?
ER... NO...
I JUST REALISED SOMETHING... CREUTZFELD, IN GERMAN, LITERALLY MEANS...
"FIELD OF CROSSES"...

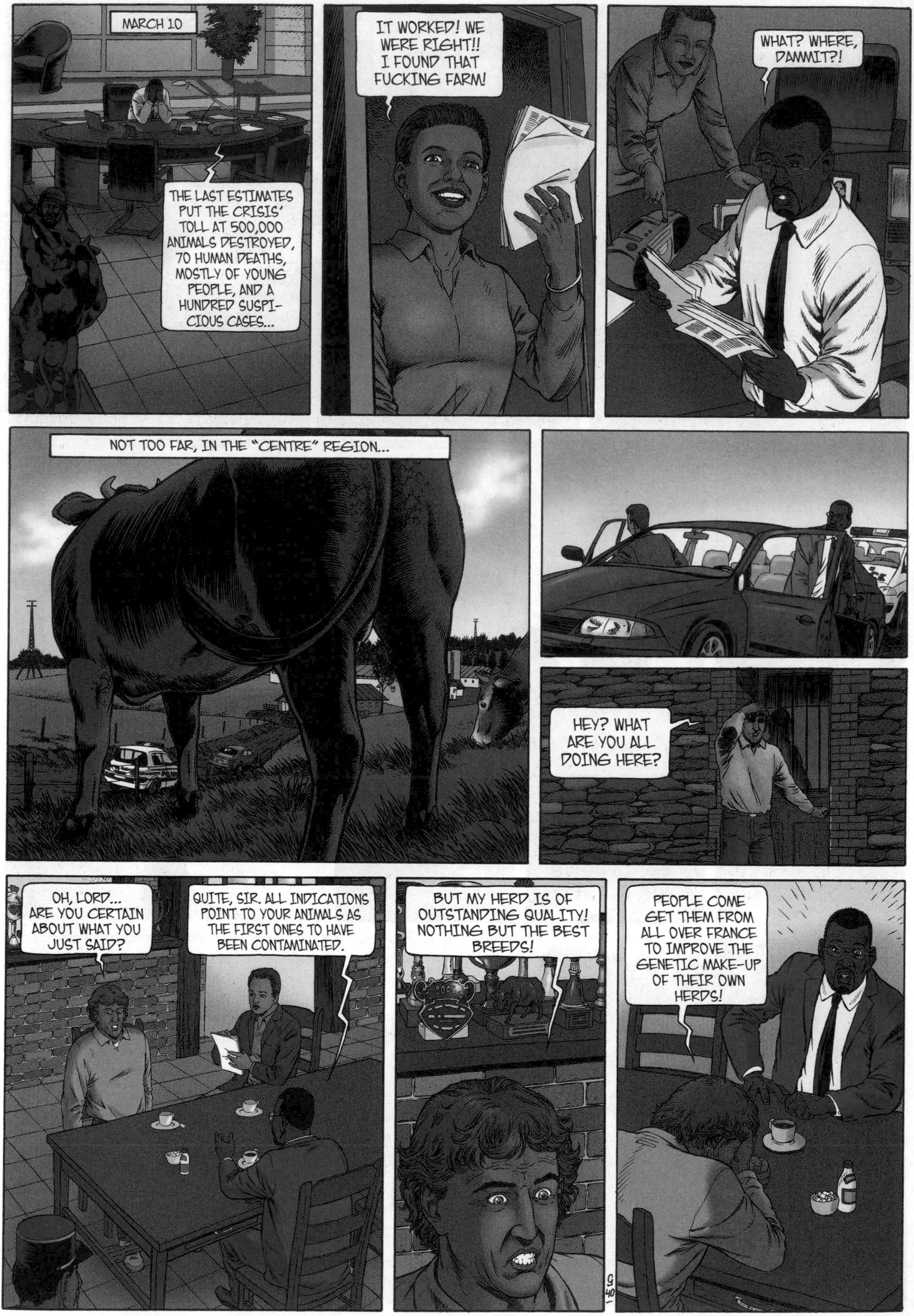
MARCH 10
THE LAST ESTIMATES PUT THE CRISIS' TOLL AT 500,000 ANIMALS DESTROYED, 70 HUMAN DEATHS, MOSTLY OF YOUNG PEOPLE, AND A HUNDRED SUSPI-CIOUS CASES...
IT WORKED! WE WERE RIGHT!! I FOUND THAT FUCKING FARM!
WHAT? WHERE, DAMMIT?!
NOT TOO FAR, IN THE "CENTRE" REGION...
HEY? WHAT ARE YOU ALL DOING HERE?
OH, LORD... ARE YOU CERTAIN ABOUT WHAT YOU JUST SAID?
QUITE, SIR. ALL INDICATIONS POINT TO YOUR ANIMALS AS THE FIRST ONES TO HAVE BEEN CONTAMINATED.
BUT MY HERD IS OF OUTSTANDING QUALITY! NOTHING BUT THE BEST BREEDS!
PEOPLE COME GET THEM FROM ALL OVER FRANCE TO IMPROVE THE GENETIC MAKE-UP OF THEIR OWN HERDS!

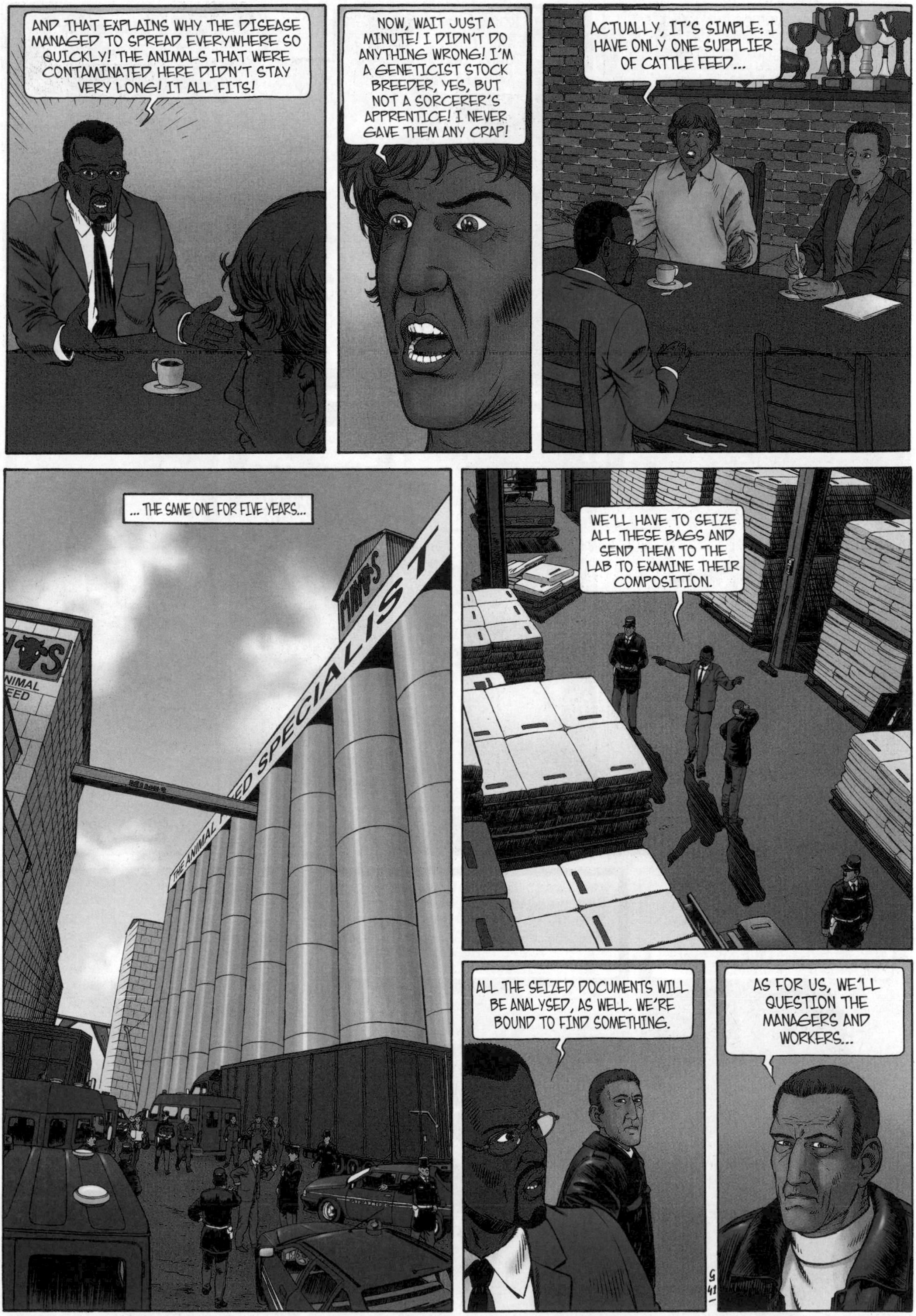
AND THAT EXPLAINS WHY THE DISEASE MANAGED TO SPREAD EVERYWHERE SO QUICKLY! THE ANIMALS THAT WERE CONTAMINATED HERE DIDN'T STAY VERY LONG! IT ALL FITS!
NOW, WAIT JUST A MINUTE! I DIDN'T DO ANYTHING WRONG! I'M A GENETICIST STOCK BREEDER, YES, BUT NOT A SORCERER'S APPRENTICE! I NEVER GAVE THEM ANY CRAP!
ACTUALLY, IT'S SIMPLE: I HAVE ONLY ONE SUPPLIER OF CATTLE FEED...
... THE SAME ONE FOR FIVE YEARS...
WE'LL HAVE TO SEIZE ALL THESE BAGS AND SEND THEM TO THE LAB TO EXAMINE THEIR COMPOSITION.
ALL THE SEIZED DOCUMENTS WILL BE ANALYSED, AS WELL. WE'RE BOUND TO FIND SOMETHING.
AS FOR US, WE'LL QUESTION THE MANAGERS AND WORKERS...

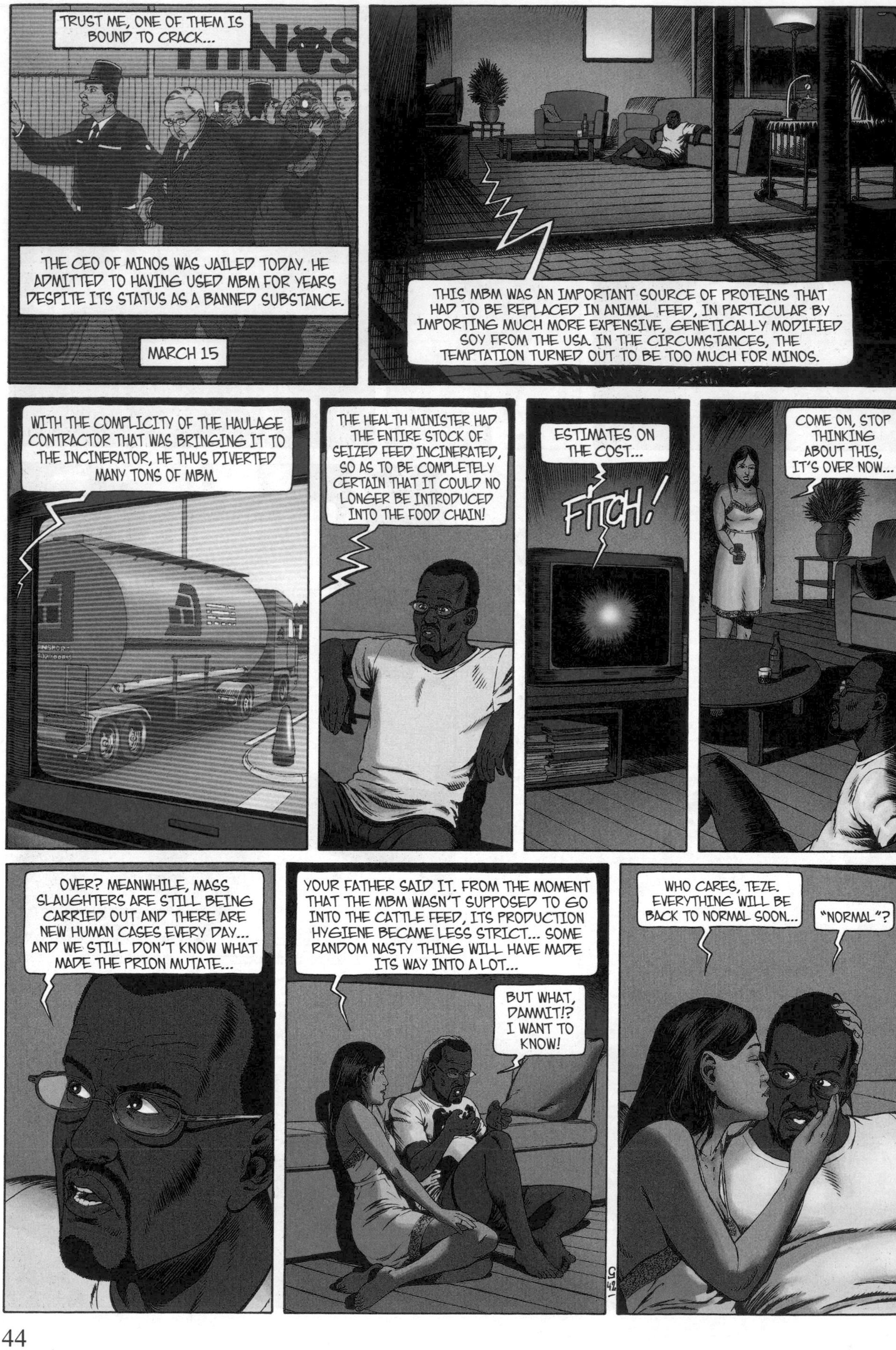
TRUST ME, ONE OF THEM IS BOUND TO CRACK...
THE CEO OF MINOS WAS JAILED TODAY. HE ADMITTED TO HAVING USED MBM FOR YEARS DESPITE ITS STATUS AS A BANNED SUBSTANCE.
MARCH 15
THIS MBM WAS AN IMPORTANT SOURCE OF PROTEINS THAT HAD TO BE REPLACED IN ANIMAL FEED, IN PARTICULAR BY IMPORTING MUCH MORE EXPENSIVE, GENETICALLY MODIFIED SOY FROM THE USA. IN THE CIRCUMSTANCES, THE TEMPTATION TURNED OUT TO BE TOO MUCH FOR MINOS.
WITH THE COMPLICITY OF THE HAULAGE CONTRACTOR THAT WAS BRINGING IT TO THE INCINERATOR, HE THUS DIVERTED MANY TONS OF MBM.
THE HEALTH MINISTER HAD THE ENTIRE STOCK OF SEIZED FEED INCINERATED, SO AS TO BE COMPLETELY CERTAIN THAT IT COULD NO LONGER BE INTRODUCED INTO THE FOOD CHAIN!
ESTIMATES ON THE COST...
FITCH!
COME ON, STOP THINKING ABOUT THIS, IT'S OVER NOW...
OVER? MEANWHILE, MASS SLAUGHTERS ARE STILL BEING CARRIED OUT AND THERE ARE NEW HUMAN CASES EVERY DAY... AND WE STILL DON'T KNOW WHAT MADE THE PRION MUTATE...
YOUR FATHER SAID IT. FROM THE MOMENT THAT THE MBM WASN'T SUPPOSED TO GO INTO THE CATTLE FEED, ITS PRODUCTION HYGIENE BECAME LESS STRICT... SOME RANDOM NASTY THING WILL HAVE MADE ITS WAY INTO A LOT...
BUT WHAT, DAMMIT!? I WANT TO KNOW!
WHO CARES, TEZE. EVERYTHING WILL BE BACK TO NORMAL SOON...
"NORMAL"?

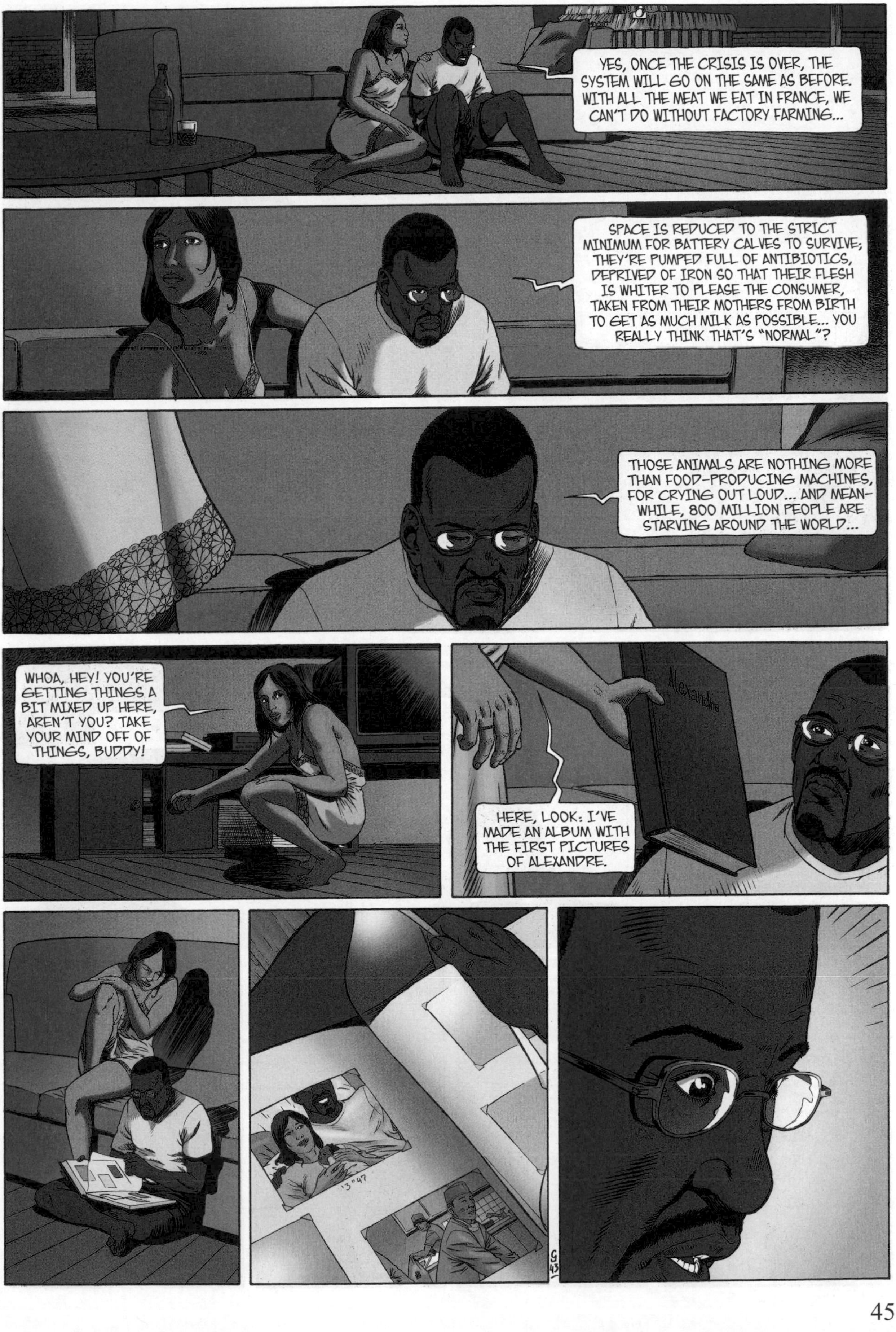
YES, ONCE THE CRISIS IS OVER, THE SYSTEM WILL GO ON THE SAME AS BEFORE. WITH ALL THE MEAT WE EAT IN FRANCE, WE CAN'T DO WITHOUT FACTORY FARMING...
SPACE IS REDUCED TO THE STRICT MINIMUM FOR BATTERY CALVES TO SURVIVE; THEY'RE PUMPED FULL OF ANTIBIOTICS, DEPRIVED OF IRON SO THAT THEIR FLESH IS WHITER TO PLEASE THE CONSUMER, TAKEN FROM THEIR MOTHERS FROM BIRTH TO GET AS MUCH MILK AS POSSIBLE... YOU REALLY THINK THAT'S "NORMAL"?
THOSE ANIMALS ARE NOTHING MORE THAN FOOD-PRODUCING MACHINES, FOR CRYING OUT LOUD... AND MEAN-WHILE, 800 MILLION PEOPLE ARE STARVING AROUND THE WORLD...
WHOA, HEY! YOU'RE GETTING THINGS A BIT MIXED UP HERE, AREN'T YOU? TAKE YOUR MIND OFF OF THINGS, BUDDY!
Alexandre
HERE, LOOK: I'VE MADE AN ALBUM WITH THE FIRST PICTURES OF ALEXANDRE.

A FEW DAYS LATER...

SO YOU FINALLY UNDERSTOOD THE WHOLE THING...

YES...

BUT... HOW?

THE NEWBORNS' PLACENTAS...

... ENDED UP IN THE COWS' FOOD, DAMMIT!!

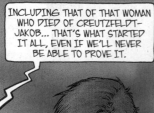

INCLUDING THAT OF THAT WOMAN WHO DIED OF CREUTZFELDT-JAKOB... THAT'S WHAT STARTED IT ALL, EVEN IF WE'LL NEVER BE ABLE TO PROVE IT.

AND YOU KNEW IT... YOU KNEW ALL THAT...

I NOSED AROUND IN THE FILES SEIZED FROM MINOS, AND I FOUND THE TRACE OF THE TRANSFER TO YOUR ACCOUNT THREE YEARS AGO. AN ENORMOUS AMOUNT—A SO-CALLED "CONSULTING FEE"... YEAH, RIGHT!

IT WAS THE PRICE OF YOUR COMPLICITY!

NO, IT'S NOT WHAT YOU THINK!

THREE YEARS AGO, I OVERHEARD THE MAN IN CHARGE OF WASTE MANAGEMENT AT THE MATERNITY HOSPITAL. HE'S THE ONE WHO'S AT THE ROOT OF EVERYTHING. I DID MY OWN INVESTIGATION...

AND, YES, I DISCOVERED EVERYTHING... THAT MINOS WAS GETTING NOT ONLY MBM FROM THAT HAULAGE CONTRACTOR, BUT ALSO HUMAN PLACENTA, TO USE AS A PROTEIN SOURCE. IT WAS COSTING THEM A LOT LESS.

INCLUDING ALL FIVE HOSPITALS IN YOUR MATERNITY NETWORK, WE'RE TALKING ABOUT 10 TONNES OF PLACENTAS PER YEAR... YOU HAD ALL THE STOCKS AT MINOS BURNED SO THAT NO ONE WOULD FIND TRACES OF HUMAN DNA THERE!!!

WE WERE CRIPPLED WITH FINANCIAL PROBLEMS. SO, I BLACKMAILED MINOS. AND I REINJECTED ALL OF THAT MONEY TO SAVE THE MATERNITY HOSPITALS! I DIDN'T PUT A SINGLE CENT IN MY OWN POCKET!

BUT YOU DID NOTHING TO PREVENT ALL OF THIS!

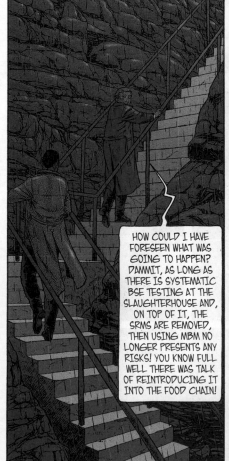

HOW COULD I HAVE FORESEEN WHAT WAS GOING TO HAPPEN? DAMMIT, AS LONG AS THERE IS SYSTEMATIC BSE TESTING AT THE SLAUGHTERHOUSE AND, ON TOP OF IT, THE SRMS ARE REMOVED, THEN USING MBM NO LONGER PRESENTS ANY RISKS! YOU KNOW FULL WELL THERE WAS TALK OF REINTRODUCING IT INTO THE FOOD CHAIN!

WHEN I HEARD THAT A WOMAN WHO HAD GIVEN BIRTH IN ONE OF OUR HOSPITALS HAD DIED OF C.J. DISEASE, I WORRIED. BUT IT WAS MUCH TOO LATE... THERE WAS NOTHING WE COULD DO. WHEN SUSPICIOUS CASES STARTING APPEARING IN COWS, I FEARED FOR THE WORST... BUT I DID EVERYTHING THEN TO STOP THE CRISIS. YOU SAW THAT YOURSELF!!!

I READ THE REPORT YOU'RE SUPPOSED TO GIVE THE PARLIAMENTARY COMMISSION OF INQUIRY. AS SUCH, IT IS DAMNING TO ME.

BUT AM I REALLY THAT GUILTY...?

47

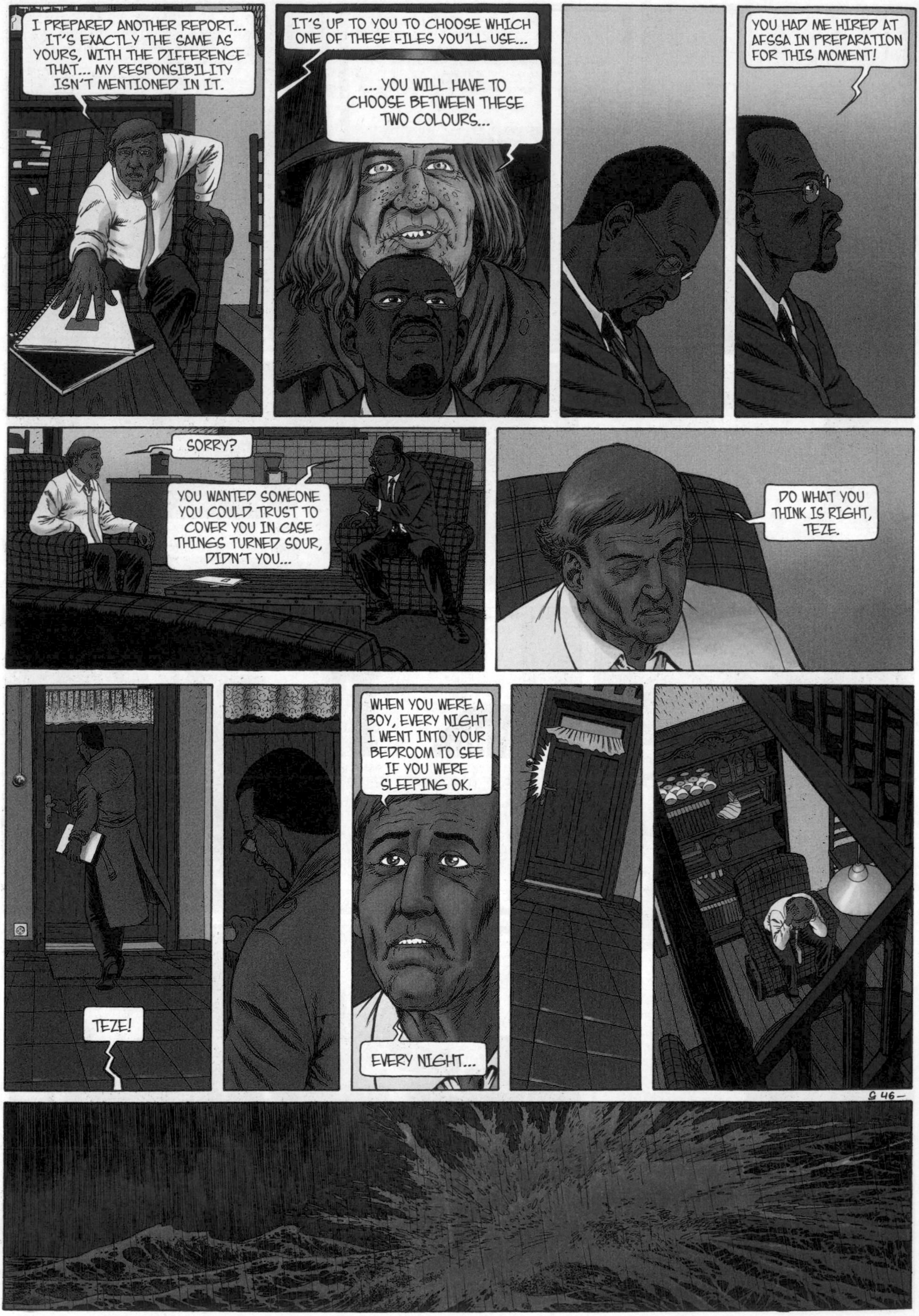

I PREPARED ANOTHER REPORT... IT'S EXACTLY THE SAME AS YOURS, WITH THE DIFFERENCE THAT... MY RESPONSIBILITY ISN'T MENTIONED IN IT.
IT'S UP TO YOU TO CHOOSE WHICH ONE OF THESE FILES YOU'LL USE...
... YOU WILL HAVE TO CHOOSE BETWEEN THESE TWO COLOURS...
YOU HAD ME HIRED AT AFSSA IN PREPARATION FOR THIS MOMENT!
SORRY?
YOU WANTED SOMEONE YOU COULD TRUST TO COVER YOU IN CASE THINGS TURNED SOUR, DIDN'T YOU...
DO WHAT YOU THINK IS RIGHT, TEZE.
TEZE!
WHEN YOU WERE A BOY, EVERY NIGHT I WENT INTO YOUR BEDROOM TO SEE IF YOU WERE SLEEPING OK.
EVERY NIGHT...

MARCH 23. HEARING OF
THE PARLIAMENTARY COMMISSION
OF INQUIRY

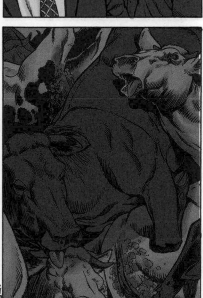

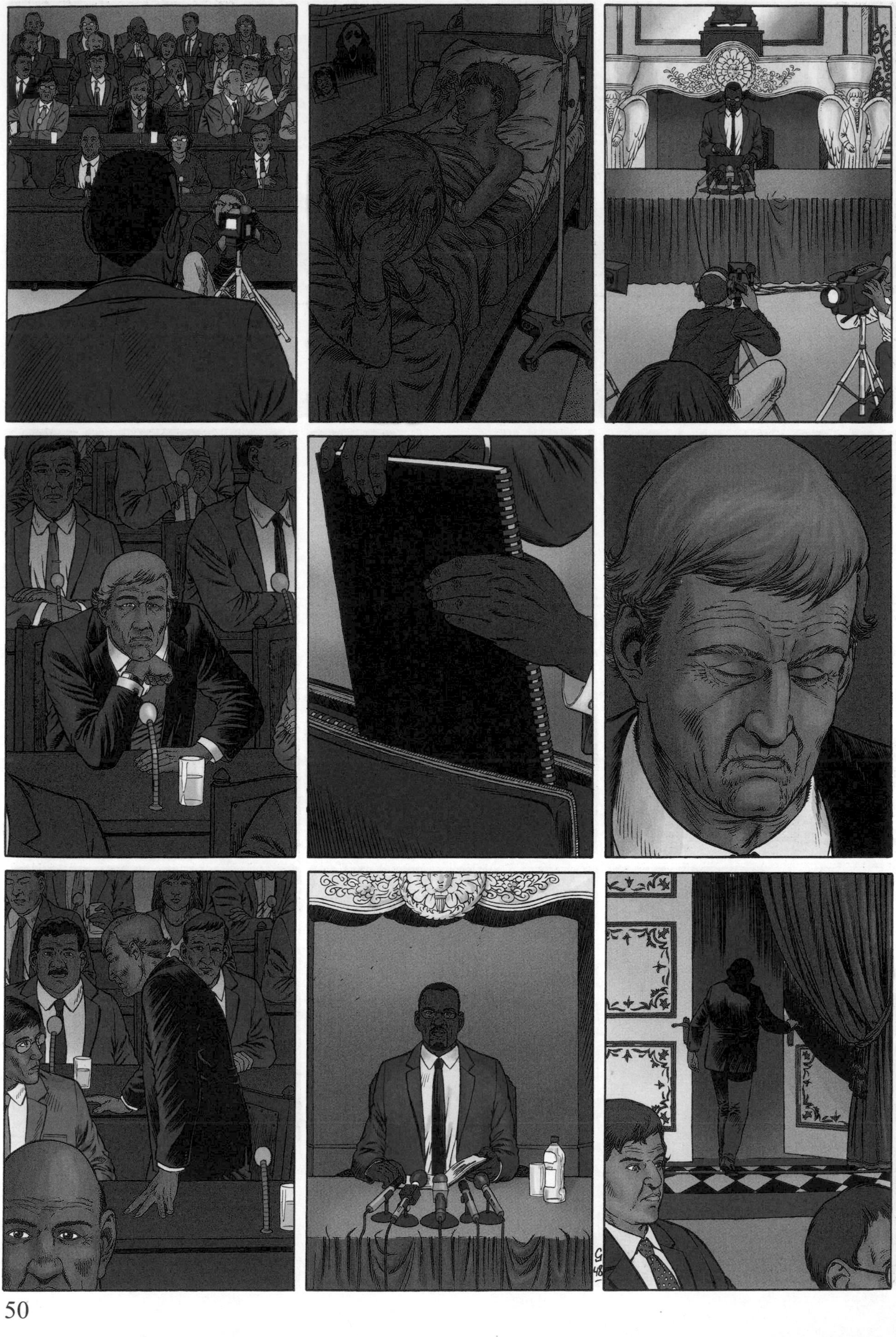

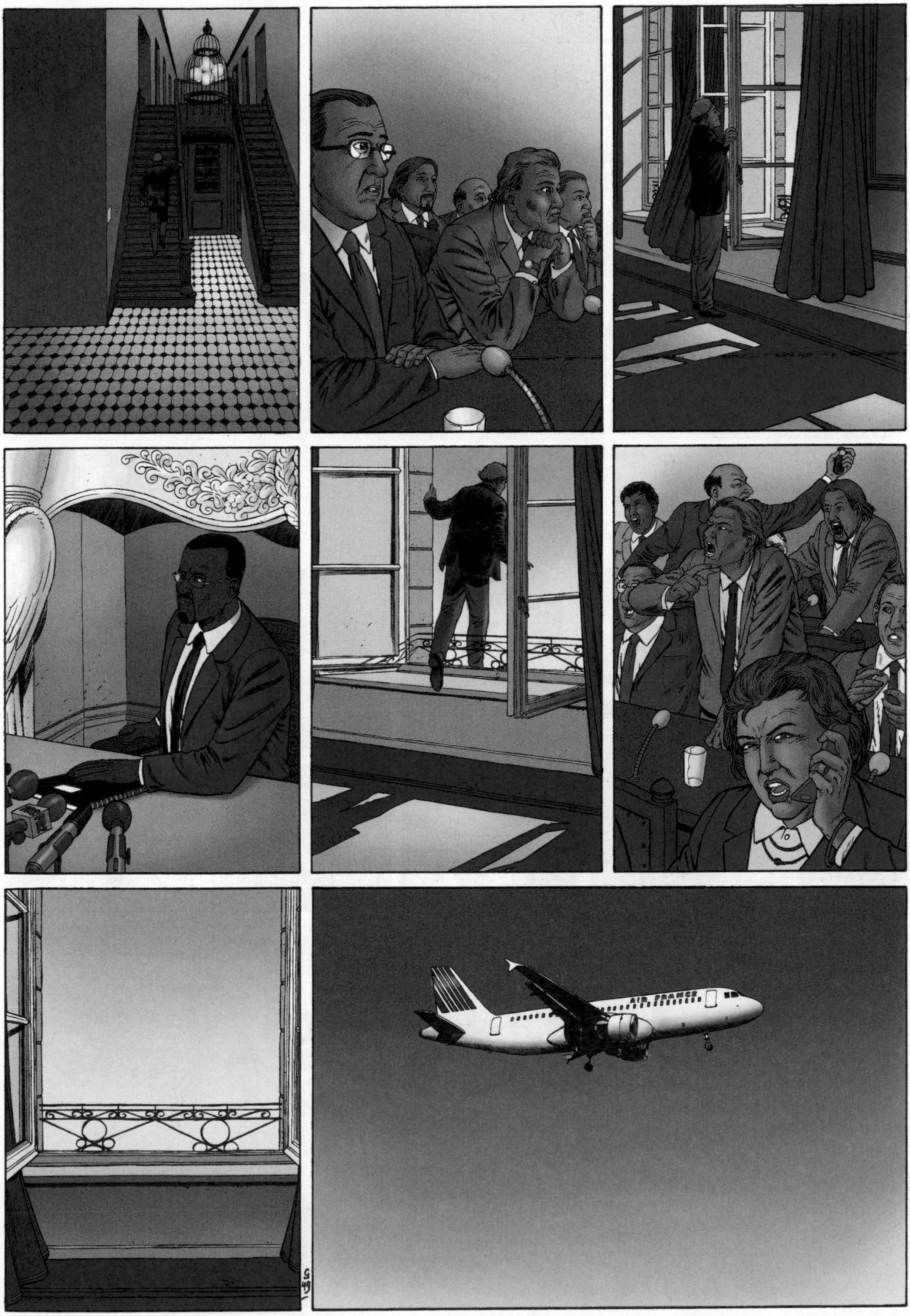
AIR FRANCE

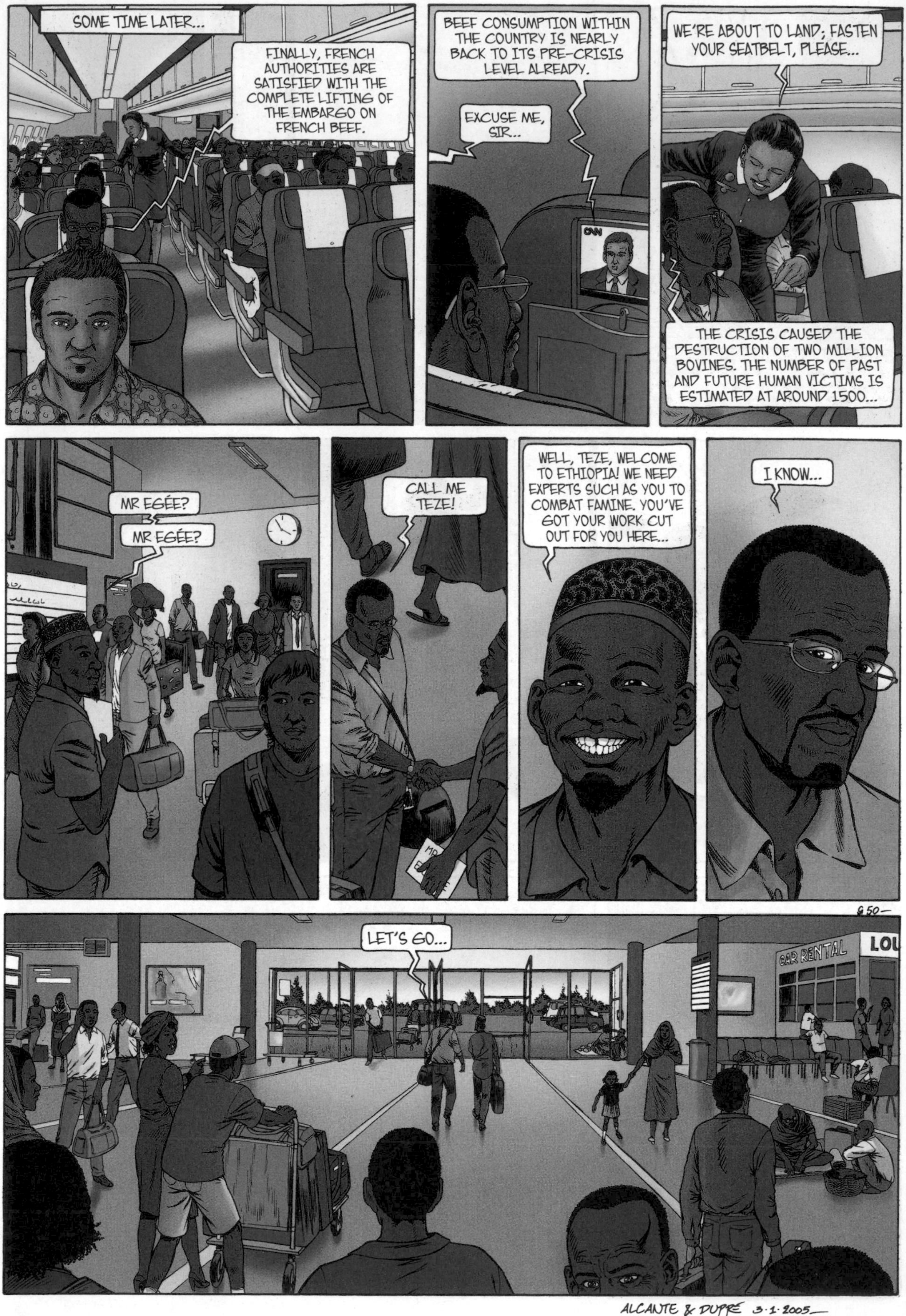
SOME TIME LATER...
FINALLY, FRENCH AUTHORITIES ARE SATISFIED WITH THE COMPLETE LIFTING OF THE EMBARGO ON FRENCH BEEF.
BEEF CONSUMPTION WITHIN THE COUNTRY IS NEARLY BACK TO ITS PRE-CRISIS LEVEL ALREADY.
EXCUSE ME, SIR...
CNN
WE'RE ABOUT TO LAND; FASTEN YOUR SEATBELT, PLEASE...
THE CRISIS CAUSED THE DESTRUCTION OF TWO MILLION BOVINES. THE NUMBER OF PAST AND FUTURE HUMAN VICTIMS IS ESTIMATED AT AROUND 1500...
MR EGÉE?
MR EGÉE?
CALL ME TEZE!
WELL, TEZE, WELCOME TO ETHIOPIA! WE NEED EXPERTS SUCH AS YOU TO COMBAT FAMINE. YOU'VE GOT YOUR WORK CUT OUT FOR YOU HERE...
I KNOW...
LET'S GO...
CAR RENTAL
LOU
ALCANTE & DUPRÉ 3·1·2005